The Earth Cries Out

Ecology and Justice

An Orbis Series on Integral Ecology

Advisory Board Members
Mary Evelyn Tucker
John A. Grim
Leonardo Boff
Sean McDonagh

The Orbis Series on Integral Ecology publishes books seeking to integrate an understanding of Earth's interconnected life systems with sustainable social, political, and economic systems that enhance the Earth community. Books in the series concentrate on ways to

- Reexamine human–Earth relations in light of contemporary cosmological and ecological science.
- Develop visions of common life marked by ecological integrity and social justice.
- Expand on the work of those exploring such fields as integral ecology, climate justice, Earth law, ecofeminism, and animal protection.
- Promote inclusive participatory strategies that enhance the struggle of Earth's poor and oppressed for ecological justice.
- Deepen appreciation for dialogue within and among religious traditions on issues of ecology and justice.
- Encourage spiritual discipline, social engagement, and the transformation of religion and society toward these ends.

Viewing the present moment as a time for fresh creativity and inspired by the encyclical *Laudato Si'*, the series seeks authors who speak to ecojustice concerns and who bring into this dialogue perspectives from the Christian communities, from the world's religions, from secular and scientific circles, or from new paradigms of thought and action.

THE EARTH CRIES OUT

*How Faith Communities Meet
the Challenges of Sustainability*

GARY GARDNER

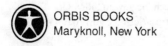

ORBIS BOOKS
Maryknoll, New York

Founded in 1970, Orbis Books endeavors to publish works that enlighten the mind, nourish the spirit, and challenge the conscience. The publishing arm of the Maryknoll Fathers and Brothers, Orbis seeks to explore the global dimensions of the Christian faith and mission, to invite dialogue with diverse cultures and religious traditions, and to serve the cause of reconciliation and peace. The books published reflect the views of their authors and do not represent the official position of the Maryknoll Society. To learn more about Orbis Books, please visit our website at www.orbisbooks.com.

Copyright © 2021 by GreenFaith
Published by Orbis Books, P.O. Box 302, Maryknoll, NY 10545-0302.
All rights reserved.
The Scripture quotations contained herein are from the New Revised Standard Version: Catholic Edition, Copyright © 1989 and 1993, by the Division of Christian Education of the National Council of the Churches of Christ in the United States of America. Used by permission. All rights reserved.
No part of this publication may be reproduced or transmitted in any form or by any means, electronic or mechanical, including photocopying, recording, or any information storage or retrieval system, without prior permission in writing from the publisher.
Queries regarding rights and permissions should be addressed to: Orbis Books, P.O. Box 302, Maryknoll, NY 10545-0302.
Manufactured in the United States of America

Library of Congress Cataloging-in-Publication Data

Names: Gardner, Gary (Writer on sustainable development), author.
Title: The earth cries out : how faith communities meet the challenges of sustainability / Gary Gardner.
Description: Maryknoll, New York : Orbis Books, 2021. | Includes bibliographical references and index. | Summary: "The Earth Cries Out describes best practices in religious responses to the impending climate and sustainability emergency, and presents the next steps for faith communities in the years ahead"—Provided by publisher.
Identifiers: LCCN 2020049836 (print) | LCCN 2020049837 (ebook) | ISBN 9781626984110 (trade paperback) | ISBN 9781608338757 (epub)
Subjects: LCSH: Sustainable development—Religious aspects—Catholic Church. | Sustainability. | Human ecology—Religious aspects—Catholic Church. | Catholic Church. Pope (2013- : Francis). Laudato si'.
Classification: LCC BX1795.S87 G37 2021 (print) | LCC BX1795.S87 (ebook) | DDC 261.8/8—dc23
LC record available at https://lccn.loc.gov/2020049836
LC ebook record available at https://lccn.loc.gov/2020049837

To those who grasp the odds we face
yet press on,
fired by a faith and a vision
that promise a better world.

Contents

Acknowledgments

A host of people were helpful to me in completing this project. I am very grateful to Fletcher Harper and colleagues at Green-Faith for the time and support they offered. Fletcher generously freed up time and gave me wide latitude to complete the project. Neddy Astudillo, Caroline Bader, Deb Convery, Fletcher Harper, Martin Kopp, and abby mohaupt pointed me to a rich set of story possibilities for the book.

A number of people sat for interviews, commented on chapters, or otherwise gave generously of their time and expertise. I am grateful to Kathleen Bashian, Steve Bogus, Janet Broderick, Peter Buck, Molly Burhans, Stephen Capobres, Brenda Craine, Imran Dhanji, Chester France, Katharine Hayhoe, Ken Himes, Kat Hoenke, Bill Jacobs, Robert Kloska, Beth Koprowski, Thane Kriener, Bill Larme, Veit Laser, Dan Last, Thomas Loya, Erin Mackey, Mike Melara, Dan Misleh, David Mog, Robert More, Laura Morosini, Dan Morrissey, Simon Nicholson, Mary O'Brien, Dean Robinson, Julia Rocchi, Ed Sabo, Anne-Sophie Serrurier, Pat Siemen, Susan Sklar, Becca Stevens, Bob Sutherland, Mary Evelyn Tucker, Keith Warner, and Irene Woodard. I am especially grateful to Sharon Malley, a fellow parishioner at Our Lady, Queen of Peace, who read and commented intelligently on the entire manuscript.

I am also grateful to Paul McMahon, my editor at Orbis, who shepherded the manuscript to completion with skill and kindness.

Finally, I acknowledge with gratitude the religious who have taught me: the Jesuits who brought my faith to adulthood; the Franciscans who revealed God to me through creation; and the Holy Cross Sisters, Fathers, and Brothers, who live a robust commitment to marginalized people. Their lessons provided the energy for this project.

Finally, I send deep thanks to my wife, Sally, and our daughter, Clara, for their forbearance and good cheer as I worked on the book. The time and space they granted me was indispensable to completing this work and remains a debt unpaid! I am also grateful for our son, Sam, whose spirit and good humor accompanied me throughout the process.

Introduction

Generations alive today take our seats on a deeply troubled planet at a unique point in human history. The unsustainable "take, make, and waste" economic model in place since the Industrial Revolution is severely stressed, threatening the biological stability of our planet and the lives and livelihoods of millions of people. Demands for sustainable economies grow ever louder, yet agreement on a path forward is elusive. Governments and societies seem paralyzed, even as dangerous environmental and social thresholds continue to be crossed.

Fortunately, people of faith, alongside our secular brothers and sisters, are increasingly active in building sustainable societies, from myriad grassroots initiatives like those found at GreenFaith and Interfaith Power and Light to institutional efforts such as Pope Francis's 2015 encyclical, *Laudato Si'*, which challenges all people to hear "the cry of the Earth and the cry of the poor." Faith involvement brings unique and arguably indispensable contributions to the issue of sustainability. This volume imagines how emerging faith experiments, each with a bearing on sustainability, might respond robustly to Francis's call. It is written for people of faith who may be confused by the record storms, droughts, and other environmental dislocations assailing societies everywhere; who question how those changes relate to their faith; and who wonder what this historic moment is asking of them.

The Urgency of Now

Until the last two centuries, no generation in ten thousand years of settled human existence had created morally problematic global-scale disruptions to life and planetary systems. We and our immediate forebears have done so. The first chapter and Parts II through IV detail the extent of these global problems. But for now, consider:

- When human activities change our planet's climate; cause extinctions that erase epochs of creative evolution; acidify the oceans and fish them to exhaustion; drain groundwater critical to food supplies; cause deserts to advance and forests to recede; erode and salinize the soils that nourish us; and generate, as a matter of course, an Asian brown cloud, a Great Pacific Garbage Patch, aquatic dead zones along six continents, and a giant hole in our atmosphere's ozone—*when these things are ordinary and accepted as "the price of progress"*—something is profoundly amiss in our relationship with the Earth.[1]

1. The Intergovernmental Panel on Climate Change (IPCC), "Summary for Policymakers," in *Global Warming of 1.5°C.*, 2018, https://www.ipcc.ch; IUCN 2020, *The IUCN Red List of Threatened Species. Version 2020-1*, https://www.iucnredlist.org; NOAA, "What Is Ocean Acidification?" PMEL Carbon Program, https://www.pmel.noaa.gov; Jon Lanman, "A Comprehensive Guide to Overfishing: The Facts, Causes, and Solutions," *Exo*, August 20, 2019; USGS, "Groundwater Decline and Depletion," https://www.usgs.gov; M. Cherlet et al., eds., *World Atlas of Desertification* (Luxembourg: Publication Office of the European Union, 2018); Frances Seymour, "Deforestation Is Accelerating, Despite Mounting Efforts to Protect Tropical Forests. What Are We Doing Wrong?," World Resources Institute blog, https://www.wri.org; FAO and ITPS, *Status of the World's Soil Resources (SWSR)—Main Report* (Rome: Food and Agriculture Organization of the United Nations and Intergovernmental Technical Panel on Soils, 2015); "Asian Brown Cloud," *ScienceNetLinks*, http://sciencenetlinks.com; NOAA, "Garbage Patches," https://marinedebris.noaa.gov; Denis Breitburg et al., "Declining Oxygen in the Global Ocean and Coastal Waters," *Science*,

- And when, in an ever-wealthier world, 820 million people struggle with hunger alongside 2,100 billionaires; when an African child is twelve times more likely than an American child to die before the age of five; when climate catastrophes caused by the comfortable are projected to create tens of millions of climate refugees, *and when these outrages trigger no corrective system response,* something is profoundly amiss in our relationship with one another.[2]

These wounds to the planet and its people are widespread and interconnected, suggesting failures that are systemic, rather than isolated, in nature. Indeed, entire ecological, economic, and social systems—the foundation of industrial civilizations—are under serious stress, are at risk of collapse, and urgently need overhaul.

Certainly, the industrial model of development that began in the eighteenth century and eventually swept across most of the world has produced tremendous advances in life expectancy, health outcomes, and education, and has spurred innovations that make life comfortable and convenient for a sizable share of the human family. Many of these gains should be preserved, if possible. But these fruits are available unequally across the globe, and even fortunate populations are vulnerable as the pillars supporting our comfortable lives weaken and crack. Indeed, while many cities and civilizations shimmer with achievement, their successes will erode in the decades ahead unless we learn to overcome the twin Achilles' heels of ecological and social neglect.

The commonly cited cure for today's global economic and environmental dysfunction is sustainable development—

January 5, 2018; NASA, "NASA Data Aids Ozone Hole's Journey to Recovery," https://www.nasa.gov., April 30, 2020.

2. Luisa Kroll, "Billionaires: The Richest People in the World," *Forbes*, March 5, 2019; UNICEF, "Child Mortality Estimates," September 9, 2020.

economic activity that provides for the needs of all and unfolds within ecological boundaries. Innovative sustainability solutions exist today, ranging from renewable energy and regenerative agriculture to walkable cities and circular economies. These deserve urgent attention and commitment. But they are not enough. As chapter 2 suggests, people of faith offer a range of additional dimensions—moral and spiritual in nature—that can deepen and broaden the technological and economic solutions now on the drawing boards.

People of Faith as Changemakers

If congregations and faith institutions offer spiritual and moral underpinnings for sustainable development, they are also well positioned to offer *lived expressions* of sustainability that can help to jump-start the transition to sustainable societies. People of faith bring a set of infrastructural, social, financial, political, and of course, moral and spiritual, tools to the sustainability challenges of our time. Consider, for example, that people of faith are organized into communities that:

- meet regularly
- are motivated and guided by a vigorous moral and spiritual energy
- possess scriptural and other teachings that speak to sustainability issues
- are heirs to a long tradition of engagement on social justice issues
- understand and sometimes tap the power of prophetic voices
- can act as an influential political force when they desire to
- control meaningful amounts of investment capital
- manage land and buildings that are potential sustainability showcases

- possess the moral standing to address issues, like consumerism, that other groups avoid
- are small enough to undertake low-risk social and economic experiments, and
- are large enough, via linkages with other congregations, to move the needle on sustainability issues.

Few institutions at the global level have such a broad and powerful tool set. Of course, these assets are seldom utilized to their fullest potential; people of faith are arguably punching well below their weight on the critical issues of our day. Yet skillfully employed, these assets could help convert civilizational decline into a rejuvenation in which solidarity and ecological consciousness become ethical norms. Pope Francis calls regularly and concretely for faith activism to transform societies, challenging us to step up and make a difference. Take, for example, his 2015 pitch to members of an Italian federation of cooperatives:

> How beautiful it would be if, starting in Rome, an effective network of assistance and solidarity could be created among the cooperatives, for parishes and hospitals. . . . And the people, starting from the most needy, would be placed at the centre of . . . this solidarity movement: the people at the centre, the neediest at the centre. This is the mission we are proposing to ourselves! *It is your task to invent practical solutions.* . . .[3] (emphasis added)

In 2020, Francis announced a bold Catholic effort to jumpstart the societal transition to sustainability, the multiyear

---

3. "Address of His Holiness Pope Francis to Representatives of the Confederation of Italian Cooperatives," February 28, 2015, http://www.vatican.va.

Laudato Si' Action Platform. The program will roll out sustainability commitments and actions among a series of Catholic institutions, including families, dioceses, schools, universities, hospitals, businesses, and religious orders. Institutions will be challenged to demonstrate commitments on a range of sustainability actions, from adoption of renewable energy to simplified lifestyles and development of ecological catechesis, retreats, and prayer. The initiative is ambitious: "We hope to inspire a people's movement from below for creation care," declared a dicastery official,[4] to achieve "total sustainability" over seven years.[5] This is an astonishingly bold and speedy agenda for an institution often said to "think in centuries"!

ABOUT THIS VOLUME

Pope Francis's vision of societal conversion will require a massive change of hearts, practices, and policies. This historic moment of social and political flux poses an opportunity to rethink economies and societies at the most fundamental levels—to create clean, "no-waste" economies, for example, and economies of solidarity. This volume contains inspirations that, taken together, offer a sense of how widespread change might be jump-started. Some are long-standing but newly relevant resources, like parish credit unions. Others showcase new and exciting ideas, such as mapping church lands for their ecological and conserva-

4. Brian Roewe, "Vatican Office Invites Church on Journey to 'Total Sustainability' in Next Decade," *National Catholic Reporter,* May 17, 2020, ncronline.org.

5. Roewe, "Vatican Office Invites Church"; see also Dicastery for Promoting Integral Human Development, "Laudato Si' Special Anniversary Year, 24 May 2020–24 May 2021," May 16, 2020, http://www. humandevelopment.va.

tion value. Each inspiration is an innovation, or an innovative enlargement of established faith activities.

Part I (This Moment) lays the groundwork for the book by describing the sustainability challenges facing humanity today and the ecological conversion needed to meet those challenges. Parts II (Hearing the Cry of the Earth), III (The Consumption Connection), and IV (Hearing the Cry of the Poor) encompass nine chapters focused on sustainability issues, grouped thematically around environmental issues, consumerism, and social issues, respectively. Each part is introduced with a brief review of *Laudato Si'* to provide a backdrop of church teaching related to the chapter discussions. The nine chapters open with stories of inspired faith actions regarding the issue, followed by a sustainability challenge of that issue, and closes with a Leavenings reflection to raise and expand the chapter's innovation in achieving its fullest potential. The book concludes with two chapters that deal with speaking up and acting in favor of a sustainable civilization.

The book is not a road map for building sustainable faith institutions or sustainable economies. Nor are the nine sustainability issues covered necessarily the ones most urgently needing attention. Indeed, faith involvement in sustainability issues needs to range well beyond the nine considered here. Instead of a how-to manual on sustainability, the nine issues demonstrate the potential range and power of faith communities for jumpstarting the creation of sustainable economies and societies. The objective is to help people think creatively and confidently about their potential contributions to building new, sustainable civilizations.

More Voices, Richer Harmony

This volume, authored by a Catholic for a Catholic publisher, is also supported by GreenFaith, an interfaith environmental organization; thus the volume delights in including non-Catholic and non-Christian perspectives. One of the great blessings of this historical moment is the increased appreciation of diverse ways of viewing the world and the divine. Many readers have grown up in Christian households in predominantly Christian nations, where cultural touchstones often affirm our spiritual worldview and deepest beliefs. Blessed are we who also value, appreciate, and learn from the perspective of other, often ancient, traditions and from indigenous peoples.

Pope Francis is a helpful guide in this regard, given his pursuit of warm relations beyond Catholicism. He is close to the ecumenical patriarch Bartholomew, spiritual head of Orthodox Christians, whom he refers to as his brother. He has promoted closer ties with the Jewish people, writing in 2019 of the need "to ask for forgiveness and to repair the damage" caused by "nineteen centuries of Christian anti-Judaism."[6] The same year, he issued an unprecedented joint text with Muslims, "On Human Fraternity," entering the pavilion for the signing ceremony hand in hand with Sheikh Mohammed bin Rashid Al Maktoum, vice-president of the United Arab Emirates. Furthermore, his commitment to indigenous peoples is clear from his 2020 apostolic exhortation, *Querida Amazonia*, in which he declares that "we do not need an environmentalism that is concerned for the biome but ignores the Amazonian peoples."[7] Francis's interest in respect, encounter, and dialogue is a helpful example as global

6. Marco Cassuto Morselli and Giulio Michelini, eds., *The Friendship Bible: Passages of the Torah-Pentateuch Commented Upon by Jews and Christians* (Milan: Edizioni San Paolo, 2019).

7. Pope Francis, "*Querida Amazonia*: Post-Synodal Apostolic Exhortation

crises ramp up and multiply. "We lose nothing by engaging in dialogue," he observes. "We always gain something. In a monologue, we all lose, all of us."[8]

OUR PROSPECTS

In mid-2020, the mood was gloomy, with the COVID-19 pandemic and economic downturn stealing headlines, even as climate and other environmental catastrophes continue to unfold and as political instability rocks many national governments. A record number of people say the United States is on "the wrong track." Terms like "existential threat," "post-truth," and "unprecedented" pepper the news. People seem unmoored and frightened.

Yet we cannot afford to be pessimists or doomsayers. It is still possible that the world's governments, businesses, and societies will awaken and mobilize rapidly for an economic and societal transformation that saves us from the worst consequences of our current path. Of course, we cannot count on this, and any such transformation will require hard work on our part. But unexpected breakthroughs are possible; witness the seeming night-to-day awakening of white consciousness after the killing of George Floyd in 2020. Whatever the staying power of this budding transformation, it is surely fresh evidence that mass stirring is possible. Could a similar, wholesale conversion on climate and sustainability issues be just around the corner? Who are we to dismiss such possibility?

God promises always to accompany us. We access God's help

---

of the Holy Father Francis to the People of God and to All Persons of Good Will," February 2, 2020, 8.

8. "Address of His Holiness Pope Francis," meeting on the theme "Theology after *Veritatis Gaudium* in the Context of the Mediterranean," June 21, 2019, http://www.vatican.va.

most effectively when we listen deeply, discerning carefully the path forward. Divine guidance may point us in directions we would rather avoid, sacrificial paths of justice and environmental responsibility that require us to heed voices long ignored, especially of those groups, both human and nonhuman, that are marginalized and vulnerable. We resist, of course; we want any new civilization to be built on *our* terms. But surely we grasp by now that our insistence on control over nature, our overconfidence in human cleverness, and our excessive reliance on free-market solutions is what created our environmental and social crises in the first place. Humility and surrender are in order; through a posture of spiritual openness, we are attuned to God's beckoning and ready to receive God's help.

Many faith communities are making efforts to build new societies. They are reading the signs of the times, listening for the voice of God, and responding. No parish or congregation, no religion or denomination, no community or nation has cracked the code of sustainable living in the modern era. But faith traditions and indigenous wisdom hold guiding insights and innovations necessary to make our way forward. May their inspirations, like those highlighted in this volume, help to energize our own efforts.

Part I

This Moment

1

Signs of the Times

Pick up any newspaper or listen to any broadcast, and the headlines provide a fresh batch of events: leaders elected, catastrophes suffered, legislation passed, the powerful humbled. Each day brings novelty—which is why we call it the news.

Imagine, instead, if the news featured not the most *novel* information but the most *important*. Headlines would shout a different set of truths, and some might run repeatedly, for days, years, and even decades on end:

"Global Temperature Up Again as Earth's Carbon Blanket Thickens"

"Species Continue Mass Die-Off, the First Caused by Humans"

"Zip Codes Can Predict a Person's Life Prospects"

"Aquifers Overpumped in Key Farm Regions; Critical Resource Continues to be Drained"

"Eight Richest People Have as Much Wealth as Poorest Half of Humanity"

Jaw-dropping developments like these are not new on any given day; each describes processes underway for decades or longer. Yet they merit daily attention and action because they are "signs of the times"—Jesus's term for societal markers of moral importance. The would-be headlines cited above are steeped in moral content: a degraded Earth represents the desecration of creation, and neglect of our suffering kin is a fundamental offense in the eyes of God. Indeed, humanity's seeming willingness to spoil the gift of creation and to ignore the poorest among us reveals a moral culpability of biblical proportions. Now *that* should make headlines!

The moral character of today's signs of the times deepens further given the many warnings spread over half a century of humanity's steadily worsening damage to the planet. Hundreds of conferences and reports could be cited but consider the series of warnings issued by world scientists since 1992. In the first "World Scientists' Warning to Humanity," 1,700 scientists laid out the dangers posed by the unsustainable practices of industrial economies. The warning attracted media attention but little substantive response, so 20,000 scientists issued a second warning in 2017 that lamented the inaction and repeated the warning with greater urgency.[1] In a third appeal, which focused on the climate emergency, the scientists spoke plainly, declaring that the climate crisis had arrived, was more severe than expected, and was "threatening natural ecosystems *and the fate of humanity.*" Once again, they bemoaned humanity's response: "*We have generally conducted business as usual and have largely failed to address this predicament*" (emphasis added).[2] Our failure to act calls to mind Jesus's question to a crowd: "Why do you not know how to interpret the present time?" (Luke 12:56).

---

1. William J. Ripple et al., "World Scientists' Warning to Humanity: A Second Notice," *BioScience* 67, no. 12 (2017).

2. William J. Ripple et al., "World Scientists' Warning of a Climate Emergency," *BioScience* 70, no. 1 (2020), 8–12.

Four Characteristics

Four overarching characteristics reveal the critical importance of today's sustainability challenges. The environmental and social signs of the times, all driven by human activity, are massive, unprecedented, connected, and dangerous. Each characteristic, and certainly all taken together, suggests that humanity's presence on our planet is huge. We can even assert that on Earth our species is *dominant*—a word whose root means "lord" or "master." Therein lies the problem: humanity's posture before the natural world is one of control, of lording over, of playing the master, rather than one of mutuality, humility, and gratitude. Let's review briefly these four environmental and social characteristics that describe humanity's dominance of planet Earth and drive today's global sustainability crisis.

Massive. Many forms of environmental degradation and resource depletion are now essentially borderless. Climate change, species loss, and the ozone hole are fully global phenomena, even if they manifest differently from place to place. Sea-level rise and ocean acidification—spinoffs of climate change—are also global. Other issues manifest independently at different places on Earth, but their occurrence on every inhabited continent makes them effectively global. These include water scarcity, soil erosion, deforestation, and air pollution. In ways never seen in human history, humanity's impact is effectively planet-sized.

A tool called the "ecological footprint" gives a helpful approximation of humanity's global environmental imprint. The Global Footprint Network uses the tool to demonstrate that humanity is overconsuming the Earth: our demand for our planet's biologically productive area is 75 percent greater than the planet can provide on an ongoing basis. In other words, we would need 1.75 Earths to meet humanity's current demand for biological area into the indefinite future.[3] We get away with this overconsumption by overdrawing nature's savings accounts—for example, by cutting forests faster than they regrow or pumping wells faster than they are recharged by rainfall. But as with any savings account, continued raiding of our biological reserves will bring a day of reckoning.[4]

So large is humanity's impact on the Earth that a working group of geologists has declared a new epoch of Earth history, the Anthropocene.[5] They mark the beginning of this new epoch at the mid-twentieth century, when humanity's traces on the geology of the planet, such as the presence of radioactive elements in sediments, became widespread. Not coincidentally, mid-century is also the start of the Great Acceleration, when humanity's voracious appetite for resources of all kinds—from fuels and fertilizer to building materials and food—took off and expanded our footprint. This extraordinary demand for disposable materials—many having one-time use before being thrown away—has created the environmental damage that is altering our planet's critical operating systems.

Meanwhile, poverty can also be described as massive, especially relative to the real potential for eliminating it. Indeed, while the absolute number of poor is large—for example, one out of ten people on the planet is chronically hungry—the real scandal is that poverty continues to exist in a world of growing wealth. As chapter 7 reports, by one measure half of the world is now middle class as wealth spreads. In ancient times,

3. Global Footprint Network, "Ecological Footprint," https://www.footprintnetwork.org.

4. Global Footprint Network, "Earth Overshoot Day," https://www.footprintnetwork.org.

5. Anthropocene Working Group, "Results of Binding Vote by AWG," Subcommission on Quaternary Stratigraphy, International Commission on Stratigraphy, May 21, 2019, http://quaternary.stratigraphy.org.

the Hebrew prophets, Jesus, and other leaders were scathing in their criticism of indifference to the poor—at a time when the limited possibilities for generating wealth and well-being made poverty commonplace. How much sharper would their voices be today in a world of abundant resources, knowledge, and technology that make a dignified life for all people a real possibility, yet a distant hope for so many?

Unprecedented. There is nothing new under the sun (Ecclesiastes 1:9), and, indeed, it takes a certain confidence to claim that humanity's challenges in any era are unique. But never in the millions of years of our presence on this planet have human-caused environmental challenges been global in scope. Nor have they threatened serious damage to the full collection of human societies. Yet both characteristics are true today. The planetary changes wrought by human activities have no precedent, a humbling and daunting reality for any of our species to contemplate.

Perhaps the most shocking fact in all the literature on sustainability is that humans are driving a mass extinction of species, only the sixth in our planet's billions of years of existence, and the first caused by humans (rather than by meteors or other external phenomena). Today, species are disappearing at an estimated ten to one hundred times the natural rate as a broad range of human activities, from farming to urban expansion to fossil-fuel use, destroy or weaken the resilience of species and their habitats.[6] The potential toll is breathtaking: more than a quarter of mammal species and 41 percent of amphibian species are threatened with extinction.[7] This unraveling of the fabric

---

6. Gerardo Ceballos, Paul R. Ehrlich, and Rodolfo Dirzo, "Biological Annihilation via the Ongoing Sixth Mass Extinction Signaled by Vertebrate Population Losses and Declines," *Proceedings of the National Academy of Sciences*, July 25, 2017, https://www.pnas.org.

7. "More Than 30,000 Species Are Threatened with Extinction," The IUCN Red List of Threatened Species, https://www.iucnredlist.org.

of life is nothing less than the decimation of billions of years of God's creative work.

Connected. Today's global sustainability challenges are often an intertwined mix of environmental, social, and economic issues; pathologies in one realm often cross into others, multiplying their impact. For example, infectious diseases are not merely public health issues but can have major side effects. COVID-19 has caused robust economies to contract more dramatically than at any time since the 1930s, and the social impact has been profound as people observed social distancing and other measures that limited contact. Similarly, the impact of climate change extends beyond weather events to the economy at large. The cost of floods, storms, and fires worldwide in 2019 and 2020 was easily in excess of $100 billion each year, and estimates of total damages from climate changes through 2050 run into the trillions of dollars.[8]

A shifting environment also leads to social disruption. Consider the causal chain leading from climate change through water supply to poverty. In many regions, mountains act as water banks, holding snow and ice in the winter and releasing it in the spring and summer thaw for use in lowland cities and farms.[9] Yet, in the Andes and other mountainous regions, glaciers are in full retreat as they melt in a warming world. At least eight of Colombia's glaciers have disappeared completely,[10] while glaciers in the Cordillera Real range in Bolivia have lost two-thirds or

---

8. Katherine Kramer and Joe Ware, "Counting the Cost 2019: A Year of Climate Breakdown," *Christian Aid*, December 2019, christianaid.org; trillions figure from Patrick Galey, "Climate Impacts 'to Cost World $7.9 Trillion' by 2050," phys.org, November 20, 2019.

9. T. Schoolmeester and K. Verbist, eds., *The Andean Glacier and Water Atlas: The Impact of Glacier Retreat on Water Resources* (Arendal, Norway: UNESCO, GRID-Arendal, 2018), 23.

10. Schoolmeester and Verbist, eds., *Andean Glacier*, 42.

more of their area over the last few decades.[11] Loss of water, a fundamental building block for urban and rural economies alike, will have major economic ramifications in western Latin America, hobbling economic activity and likely increasing poverty. Melting glaciers and their economic and social tentacles are also a serious concern in the Sierras in California and the Himalayas in South Asia.

Dangerous. Finally, humanity's large and interconnected environmental presence means that failures in one area can spread and bring great danger for the world. In 1972, a modeling study, *The Limits to Growth*, looked decades into the future and produced a series of graphs that showed trends in resources, food production, industrial output, and population growth. All moved steadily upward for fifty years or more, then turned downward in a global economic collapse over several decades in the middle of this century.[12] Actual developments have largely followed the model's upward-trending projections; now we are entering the period that the model predicted could see key trends turn downward.[13]

Other dangers come from an overloaded environment. The oceans, for example, act like a sponge in absorbing excess carbon dioxide and limiting global warming; without this service our climate predicament would be much more dire. But like any sponge, oceans have limited absorption capacity, meaning that this valuable assist will one day end, causing atmospheric

---

11. Schoolmeester and Verbist, eds., *Andean Glacier*, 46.
12. Donella H. Meadows et al., *The Limits to Growth: A Report for the Club of Rome's Project on the Predicament of Mankind* (New York: Universe Books, 1972).
13. Graham Turner, "Is Global Collapse Imminent?" MSSI Research Paper No. 4, Melbourne Sustainable Society Institute, The University of Melbourne, 2014, https://sustainable.unimelb.edu.au.

concentrations to increase and warming to accelerate.[14] Some scientists see signs that oceanic absorption of carbon dioxide has already begun to slow.[15]

Danger also lurks on the social side of this sustainability crisis. For example, we now understand that air pollution affects every major organ in the body, from birth to death, and that its health and economic impacts are greater than previously believed. Meanwhile, unequal access to land, water, and other resources often increases economic vulnerability among women and people who are poor. For example, "land grabs"—the taking of farmland by elites—can displace poor farmers and push them onto marginal land that is not only less productive but more prone to environmental damage, driving the poor into greater poverty. Differential access leads to disadvantage for marginalized groups.[16]

One might argue that the massive, unprecedented, connected, and dangerous nature of the sustainability challenge suggests that today's resource-intensive civilizations have outgrown our planet. This is new. Previous generations never worried about trespassing vital boundaries of their planet. We do, largely because our *domination* of the planet is a corruption of the *dominion* given to humanity in Genesis. What was ordained to be a harmonious mutuality between humanity and the Earth[17] has been twisted into an instrumental relationship in which our planet is humanity's supply depot and workbench.

14. Li-Qing Jiang et al., "Surface Ocean pH and Buffer Capacity: Past, Present and Future," *Nature Scientific Reports*, December 9, 2019, https://doi.org/10.1038/s41598-019-55039-4.

15. Jiang et al., "Surface Ocean pH and Buffer Capacity."

16. Melissa Leach, "Inequality and Sustainability," in *World Social Science Report 2016* (Paris: UNESCO and International Social Science Council, 2016), 132–34, https://unesdoc.unesco.org.

17. See Pope Francis, *Laudato Si': On Care for Our Common Home* (Vatican City: Libreria Editrice Vaticana, 2015), 66–67.

Despite the late hour and the enormous tangle of ominous trends, a faith-filled strategist might find reason for hope. The tight link between environmental and social pathologies, which sends us spiraling downward into worsening degradation and neglect, can be turned to our advantage. By using enlightened values to revamp our approach to energy, land use, agriculture, investments, enterprise, and other key shapers of our economies, we can initiate an upward spiral of healing for our planet and its people. The look and feel of those enlightened values are the focus of the next chapter.

2

Sustainability Plus

A commonly prescribed cure for our global predicament is "sustainable development"—the wholesale makeover of economies to favor human well-being within boundaries set by nature.[1] The bland label belies its importance; a sustainability revolution could be as momentous as the agricultural revolution that transformed hunter-gatherer bands into settled societies starting ten thousand years ago, and the Industrial Revolution that brought mind-bending advances in science, commerce, and culture starting in the eighteenth century. If successful, a sustainability revolution will feature a reclaimed understanding of economic purpose and a deep sense of mutuality with the planet on which we depend.

The sustainability revolution encompasses environmental care, certainly, but also much more. It reimagines production and consumption with dramatic reductions in waste through enhanced reuse and recycling, provision of services in place of goods, and smart design. Cities are revamped to reject sprawl, demoting the private car in urban transportation while enhancing social, cultural, and economic connection through smarter

1. This is shorthand. The classic definition of sustainable development is "development that meets the needs of the present without compromising the ability of future generations to meet their own needs." See World Commission on Environment and Development, *Our Common Future* (Oxford: Oxford University Press, 1987).

city design. Healthy soils become a central focus of agriculture, changing the look, feel, and output of farms. Energy for power, heating and cooling, and transportation comes from renewable sources. Ecological resilience is restored to land, water, and the atmosphere as the environment regains its rightful seat at the policy table. And societies commit to providing opportunity and basic services to all, rejecting extremes of wealth and poverty as evidence of fundamental societal dysfunction. In sum, sustainable societies are not the status quo with a fresh coat of paint; they are fundamentally transformed.

Adding Value

Faith-community visions of sustainability affirm the need for innovations like clean energy, regenerative agriculture, and zero-waste production systems. But many insist on grounding such innovations in the fertile terrain of values and spirituality. This is because religious leaders see the sustainability megaproblem not simply as a set of technological or policy challenges but fundamentally as a crisis of *meaning*.[2] We have lost our way environmentally and socially because we are confused about our place and purpose on this planet. This crisis of meaning, which is especially pronounced in societies that elevate consumption to the primary purpose of life, impels religious and spiritual communities to weigh in on the creation of sustainable economies and societies.[3]

Catholic thought reinjects meaning into our understanding of development by broadening the concept to embrace spiritual and moral components, a broadening that is often reflected in

2. Ilia Delio, Keith Douglass Warner, and Pamela Wood, *Care for Creation: A Franciscan Spirituality of the Earth* (Cincinnati, OH: Franciscan Media, 1999), 13.

3. Delio, Warner, and Wood, *Care for Creation*, 13.

church documents by the word "integral." Pope Paul VI's encyclical *Populorum Progressio*, for example, argues for an "integral human development" that moves beyond a narrow focus on increased income to embrace the full range of human needs and the full range of humans.[4] Likewise, Pope Francis speaks of "integral ecology" in *Laudato Si'*,[5] connecting the economic, social, cultural, and environmental dimensions of human life and setting them in the context of the common good and intergenerational justice.[6] For example, he is quick to link the climate crisis, inequality, and poverty, insisting that any climate analysis include the injustice of poor people suffering because of the excessive lifestyles of the world's richest.[7] Similarly, waste for Francis is not merely refuse, but also the broader cultural tendency to devalue the poor and the planet. Without this broadened understanding, Catholic teaching argues, advances in development will be incomplete and stilted. Although integral ecology is a Catholic expression, a broadened concept of development is also found in other cultures.

1. Spirit-Infused Development

An inspiring example of development infused with spiritual values is evident in the Sarvodaya Shramadana movement, a village-based program in Sri Lanka rooted in Buddhist values. Its goal is to create "a no poverty, no affluence, and conflict-free society." Its vision of development is basic, yet comprehensive,

---

4. Pope Paul VI, *Populorum Progressio: Encyclical Letter of Pope Paul VI on the Development of Peoples*, http://www.vatican.va.

5. Cardinal Peter Turkson, "*An Integral Ecology for an Integral Society: The Great Challenge of Our Time*," address to JPIC of Franciscans in Terra Santa Conference on the Integral Ecology of Pope Francis for the Safeguarding of Our Common Home, March 12, 2018, http://www.humandevelopment.va.

6. Jessica Ludescher Imanaka, Greg Prussia, and Samantha Alexis, "*Laudato Si'* and Integral Ecology: A Reconceptualization of Sustainability," *Journal of Management for Global Sustainability* 5, no. 1 (2017): 59.

7. Pope Francis, *Laudato Si'*, no. 25.

covering people's physical, social, and spiritual needs. For Sarvodayans, development consists of:

- a clean and beautiful environment
- a clean and adequate supply of water
- basic clothing
- a balanced diet
- a simple house to live in
- basic health care
- simple communication facilities
- basic energy requirements
- a well-rounded education
- cultural and spiritual sustenance

By including nonmaterial assets such as a beautiful environment, a well-rounded education, and cultural and spiritual sustenance, the Sarvodayan approach makes clear that environmental, social, and spiritual dimensions are all necessary for full development.[8]

In sum, faith support for sustainable development is not the mere addition of an influential voice to the global discussion; it is meant to deepen the concept of sustainability by rooting it in a broader moral and spiritual terrain that emphasizes human dignity and purpose. Pope Francis's message is that the development of people and care for the planet are integrated pieces. He insists that "we are not faced with two separate crises, one environmental and the other social, but rather one complex crisis which is both social and environmental."[9]

CALLED TO CONVERSION

Embracing integral ecology requires what Pope Francis calls an "ecological conversion"—a dramatic makeover in thinking that

---

8. Gary T. Gardner, *Inspiring Progress: Religions' Contributions to Sustainable Development* (New York: W. W. Norton, 2007), 40.

9. Pope Francis, *Laudato Si'*, no. 139.

reveals the natural world as sacred and humanity's position in it as one of kinship. No longer is nature an afterthought; no longer is humanity's voice the only one of value. The environment, so often viewed as just another policy sector on a par with the economy, education, transportation, or the arts, is now understood to be foundational, the bedrock on which economies and societies are built. An ecological conversion is deep and transformational, as revolutionary in its own way as another conversion urged by the church and familiar to many Christians, the "preferential option for the poor" (see below, 2. Option for the Poor as Christian Conversion). People who experience an ecological conversion and a preferential option for the poor are transformed; they behave in new ways, driven by love of God and neighbor—human and nonhuman.

---

2. Option for the Poor as Christian Conversion

Christians have long been urged to commit themselves to the marginalized in society, by making a "preferential option for the poor." The phrase, dating from 1968, challenges all people to prioritize care for the poor. The concept reflects the many biblical texts in which God demonstrates a particular concern for those on the margins of society. Although originating with liberation theology activists in Latin America, the term appears widely in official Catholic teaching today.

Ironically, wealthy people and societies may have the hardest time committing to an option for the poor. We who have more discretionary income may be bound to our wealth and challenged to give generously. For the comfortable, an option for the poor requires a conversion that melts hardened hearts. By contrast, stories abound of abysmally poor people who share their meager possessions with others who suffer; for them, an option for the poor is a lived, daily experience.

Ecological conversion starts with seeing and appreciating nature, exercising a muscle that may have atrophied in many modern people. Two elementary, common-sense truths can begin to restore nature to its proper place in the worldviews of industrial peoples. The first is that the natural environment is the foundation of every aspect of our lives; *everything we do*, from work to study to play, would be impossible without nature. Even spiritual pursuits, including meditation, emerge from minds and bodies nourished by the fruits of the Earth; and they are practiced in wood or stone temples or homes—or in the unmediated environment of a forest or beach. Thus, our every act, our every breath, is rooted in a supportive, cradling, spirit-infused material environment. To ignore nature is to miss this larger and richer picture that envelops and hosts our human experience. In industrialized countries, people who are challenged to absorb this perspective of intimacy with nature might turn for conversion, in humility, to early teachers of our faith traditions and to indigenous people, whose wisdom is urgently needed today.

3. Humility in Conversion

Our call to embrace the natural world is also a call to humility and repentance. As we develop an ecologically rich worldview, we learn that kinship between humans and nature is nothing new but has flourished for millennia within the world's indigenous traditions. For indigenous people, whose ties to nature are direct and intimate, the material world is infused with spirit, an understanding that, properly understood, has much to offer to industrial people. Indeed, tribes and communities long overlooked or oppressed by Western societies hold precious wisdom that industrial societies now need for survival.[10]

Such rich irony! Indigenous peoples will teach industrial peoples; non-Christians will deepen Christian thought; the

10. John A. Grim, *Indigenous Traditions and Ecology: The Interbeing of Cosmology and Community* (Cambridge, MA: Harvard University Press, 2001).

> oppressed will unbind their oppressors. Our infinitely patient and loving God corrects us through a conversion that stands our perspective on its head, humbling us as it exalts the marginalized. And in God's merciful and magnanimous wisdom, the outcome is sweet: we are all left better off.

The second obvious truth is that the physical universe predates humanity by billions of years, extending back to the Big Bang—a reality that carries deep spiritual meaning. If we ignore the story of an unfolding universe, we essentially posit that, in the disbelieving words of Franciscan Fr. Richard Rohr, "God had nothing to say" for billions of years until written Scripture appeared a few thousand years ago.[11] "Did all history prior to our sacred texts provide no basis for truth or authority?" Rohr asks. "Of course not; the radiance of the Divine Presence has been glowing and expanding since the beginning of time, before there were any human eyes to see or know about it." The long and evolving story of the universe and its importance in explaining the human story make the material world, whether at the Great Flaring Forth nearly fourteen billion years ago, or in the birds and trees that surround us today, integral to how we understand our place in creation.[12]

Enlarging Our Circle of Kin

People of faith can often look to their traditions for examples of a proper relationship with nature. For Christians, beyond our scriptural teachings, St. Francis of Assisi is an obvious choice to

11. Richard Rohr, "The Great Chain of Being," *The Mendicant* 9, no. 2 (2019): 1.

12. Brian Swimme and Thomas Berry, *The Universe Story: From the Primordial Flaring Forth to the Ecozoic Era—A Celebration of the Unfolding of the Cosmos* (San Francisco: HarperSanFrancisco, 1994), 30–45.

guide us in integrating the natural world into our faith. He is lauded for his affinity with nature, and in 2001, Pope John Paul II named him the patron saint of ecology. The designation is well deserved, but St. Francis's relationship with nature is richer and deeper than the statues and birdbaths in many Christian backyards might suggest. He was much more than a naturalist; he was an evangelist who saw creation both as God's family and as a pathway to the creator.

For St. Francis, creatures and elements were not building blocks in an edifice called "the environment." Instead, the oaks, songbirds, and wildcats of the Umbrian countryside were family to him, kin with whom he stood in relationship. This is clear in his Canticle of Creation, a song of joy that praises God through humanity's many partners in nature—Brother Sun and Sister Moon, Brother Wind and Mother Earth, for example—and for the many blessings each brings. Consider this typical verse:

> *Praised be you, my Lord*
> *through Brother Fire,*
> *by whom you light up*
> *the night, and he is*
> *handsome and merry,*
> *robust and strong.*[13]

The Canticle personalizes the elements of nature, bathing the reader in sensuous descriptions of each—Sister Moon and Stars are "lightsome and precious and fair"—as well as in depictions of the services provided; Mother Earth "sustains us and directs us, bringing forth all kinds of fruits and colored flowers and

---

13. St. Francis, "The Canticle of the Creatures," https://www.stanthony.org/the-canticle-of-the-creatures.

herbs."[14] The Canticle suggests a nature that nurtures, a relational world that envelops and sustains all who inhabit it. Readers can almost feel the warm sunshine and cleansing rivers of Umbria; it is a friendly and supportive place in Francis's telling.

Although Sister Moon, Brother Wind, and the Canticle's other natural elements grab our attention with their striking personifications, they are not the focus of the Canticle's praise. The focus is God, as each stanza makes clear: *Praised be you, my Lord.* God is praised *through* Brother Fire, *through* Sister Water; the personages of nature reflect back the beauty that God has invested in them. The rhythmic back and forth between creation and the creator—God creates and nature reflects back God's goodness—suggests that any place on Earth, at any moment in time, is an entry point to an ongoing interchange with God. Francis's poetic interpretation of creation is given powerful theological underpinnings by later thinkers. Saint Bonaventure, the Franciscan scholar and doctor of the church who lived in the decades following St. Francis's death, offered a rich theology of creation that is rooted in the Trinity (see Appendix II).

Ironically for us children of the industrial era, this thirteenth-century Franciscan thinking is revolutionary; after all, we are accustomed to seeing nature as essentially a warehouse of supplies for human projects, or a playground for our recreation. From that utilitarian perch, we could indeed mistakenly conclude that Creation Care takes a back seat in the canon of Catholic Social Teaching; we care for the environment simply because it is useful to us. But once we internalize the perspective of Francis and Bonaventure—that creation is God's self-expression, everywhere and for all time—our response can't help but be deep and rich, even awe-filled. We learn to *love* creation, we live in relation with it, and we care for it—out of deep grati-

14. https://www.stanthony.org/the-canticle-of-the-creatures.

tude, and as a return to God of the love and care that God has showered upon us. From the Franciscan perspective, Creation Care would seem to be as fundamental as breathing—a vital, ongoing part of our daily engagement with the universe and with one another.

In the twentieth century, Pierre Teilhard de Chardin and Thomas Berry set this relational perspective in the larger context of evolution. They saw the universe as alive and imbued with direction and purpose: the universe unfolds toward ever-greater complexity, characterized by an expansion of consciousness, whose purpose is union with God (see Appendix III). For these modern thinkers, humanity and nature are integral parts of an evolving world.

Pope Francis writes that protecting creation is not optional or secondary for Christians.[15] It requires the same commitment that we make in helping the poor, the hungry, the refugee, and the immigrant, and it enriches those efforts by situating them in a larger context of kinship. Rare is the Christian who feels no obligation to help the poor. Our challenge is to develop the same love and commitment toward protection of the Earth—not as an additional ethical burden but instead with the joy of a long-lost relative reunited with his extended family and feeling their loving welcome and hearty embrace. People of faith are beginning to make this commitment in innovative ways. Chapters 3 through 11 explore some of these innovations.

---

15. Pope Francis, *Laudato Si'*, no. 217.

Part II

The Cry of the Earth

Pope Francis writes in *Laudato Si'* that humanity's proper role on Earth is shaped by the concept of *relationship*: human life unfolds at the intersection of God, our neighbor, and the Earth.[1] In this web of connections, creatures and other elements of nature are not simply instruments for our use but have their own intrinsic value. "*By their mere existence* they bless him and give him glory," Francis writes, quoting the *Catechism of the Catholic Church* (emphasis added). Thus, the cry of the Earth refers to a groaning that emerges not from a sterile and distant nature, a warehouse of resources, but from brothers and sisters with whom we have a relationship of mutuality.

Our relationship with nature, says Francis, implies that humanity cannot be indifferent to the rest of creation.[2] He is critical of the human tendency to view nature in utilitarian terms, quoting the German bishops who, regarding other creatures, have written that "we can speak of the priority of *being* over that of *being useful*."[3] Indeed, far from serving merely as a tool for

---

1. Pope Francis, *Laudato Si'*, no. 66.
2. Pope Francis, *Laudato Si'*, no. 68.
3. Pope Francis, *Laudato Si'*, no. 69.

human schemes, nature is a gateway to God, revealing God's "boundless affection for us. Soil, water, mountains: everything is, as it were, a caress of God."[4]

Relationship undergirds the four chapters in this section, covering energy, food, water, and land. Each chapter features a faith-driven innovation that embraces nature in relationship to humanity and is infused with the spirit of God. In the chapter on Energy, renewables are a divine gift best deployed to serve people and conserve nature. The chapter on Water looks beyond the faucet to consider water's importance from rainfall to final use, a life cycle that serves both nature and humanity. The chapter on Food moves beyond a narrow focus on nourishment to encompass the food economy as a source of justice and environmental protections, thereby enhancing human and environmental well-being. And the chapter on Land suggests that proper management of property can heal ecosystems and better serve people.

The four topics could be supplemented with chapters on forests, oceans, mountains, and other natural realms of the entire range of nature's dimensions. Faith groups will also need to be innovative in these domains if sustainable societies are to be created. The four considered here are an initial offering on a different approach to nature that demonstrates that the cry of the Earth is increasingly being heard by people of faith.

4. Pope Francis, *Laudato Si'*, no. 84.

3

Energy

Saint Francis wrote memorably of "Brother Sun" in his Canticle of the Creatures, describing him as "handsome and merry, robust and strong." By contrast, the idiom of the solar industry today is largely techno-industrial, dominated by terms like feed-in tariffs, photovoltaics, and kilowatt-hours. (Rare is the solar engineer who speaks of Brother Sun!) Of course, the technical and economic dimensions of solar energy are important, but in the translation from medieval to modern, something valuable arguably gets lost.

For Francis, the outpouring of sunshine was a physical expression of God's abundant generosity, inviting praise and gratitude. Solar projects today could be grounded in the same spiritual soil, using an integral-ecology approach that taps the sun's rays for a broad range of benefits and ensures that each benefit is designed to advance the common good. Using such an approach, a photovoltaic installation might become a divinely inspired, multipronged development initiative pursued for the glory of God.

An inspiring example of such an approach is an innovative development initiative of Catholic Charities of the Archdiocese of Washington, DC (CCADW) that was completed in 2019. CCADW owned a seventeen-acre site in northeast Washington that was arguably underused. It consisted of a large swath of open land and an aging building used by the Missionaries of Charity, who minister to homeless people who are ill and in need of long-term care. Officials considered constructing apartments on the land, in part to generate revenue for maintenance of the sisters' building. Surely any property manager would deem the proposal a defensible one.

But was it the best *stewardship* proposal from a broad—economic, social, environmental, and spiritual—perspective? Catholic Charities teamed with Catholic Climate Covenant (CCC), a national nonprofit addressing climate and energy issues, to explore possibilities for wringing more social and economic benefit from the project while reducing the environmental impact of diocesan operations. Why not use the property to generate electricity using solar power?

CCC's affiliate, Catholic Energies, worked out a fifteen-year contract with the archdiocese to provide five thousand panels on five acres of CCADW land. The solar panels generate two megawatts of power, enough to cover the electricity needs of more than a dozen CCADW buildings across Washington. Energy savings and the lease payments from the investor that owns the system are earmarked for maintenance of the Missionaries of Charity building and contributes several hundred thousand dollars for Catholic Charities' programs.[1] Nature benefits, too: developers planted one hundred trees, which absorb carbon dioxide and improve stormwater management, and the solar field is sown not with gravel but with nectar-bearing flowers, creating a meadow that supports pollinator populations

---

1. Msgr. John Enzler, "Catholic Charities USA: Protecting the Gift of Nature Yields Win-Win for Agency," Catholic Energies, https://www. catholicenergies.org; the figure of several hundred thousand dollars is from Dan Last, email to author, June 14, 2020.

such as bees and butterflies.[2] Surplus energy from the panels is donated to Solar for All, a program in Washington that provides clean energy to low-income residents.[3]

Archbishop Wilton Gregory hastened to add the spiritual payoff: "It's not simply political, social, or economic action we're taking," he said in his blessing of the project. "We're praising God today in prayer . . . for the gift of the sun that shines on us, and more importantly, the Son that saves us."[4] Saint Francis would approve; we might imagine him expressing gratitude for the project this way:

> *Praise be to you, Lord, through Brother Sun,*
> *Who showers us with abundant energy,*
> *Who frees up riches to tend to our homeless and ill*
>   *brothers and sisters,*
> *Who inspires us to live in harmony with the rest of your*
>   *creation,*
> *Whose generosity teaches us to share with those who*
>   *have not,*
> *Who warms and nurtures the wildlife and beauty that*
>   *surrounds us*
> *Who reminds us, endlessly, of your goodness.*

Indeed, the project's broad base of environmental, social, economic, and spiritual benefits captures the integral-ecology spirit of *Laudato Si'*. Dan Misleh, the executive director of CCC, creator of Catholic Energies, and the mind behind the solar project, sees still more potential benefits if the Catholic Charities model

2. Enzler, "Catholic Charities USA: Protecting the Gift of Nature."

3. Alex Schauffler, "Celebrating the Sun That Shines on Us and the Son That Saves Us," Catholic Charities, Archdiocese of Washington, https://www.catholiccharitiesdc.org.

4. Schauffler, "Celebrating the Sun."

is replicated across the country. With degrees in theology and business, Misleh imagines the model spurring impact investing, employment for homeless people, opportunities for union laborers, and even a sharing of renewable energy across dioceses. In the process, it might showcase an inspired way, arguably a Franciscan way, to maximize the gifts given to us by God in nature.

THE CENTRAL IMPORTANCE OF ENERGY

The type of energy used in an economy shapes its society. Since the start of the Industrial Revolution in the mid-eighteenth century, industrial economies have depended heavily on fossil fuels such as coal and petroleum, powerful energy sources that can transform raw materials into an array of goods, provide light and heat, and transport people and goods quickly across vast distances. But the serious Achilles' heel of burning fossil fuels is their emission of carbon and pollutants that warm our planet and sicken its people. The need to transition to clean, renewable energy is increasingly apparent, particularly as the impacts of climate change set in. Indeed, Pope Francis, in speeches to oil company executives in 2018 and 2019, called for a "radical energy transition" away from fossil fuels, in steadily more urgent language.[5]

---

1. Speaking Truth on Energy and Climate

Addressing oil industry leaders at the Vatican in 2018, Pope Francis asserted that development cannot be achieved at the expense of the environment. "Civilization requires energy, but

---

5. Pope Francis, "Address of His Holiness Pope Francis to Participants at the Meeting Promoted by the Dicastery for Promoting Integral Human Development on the Theme: The Energy Transition & Care of Our Common Home," Vatican City, June 14, 2019, www.vatican.va.

energy use must not destroy civilization!" he declared.[6] And he critiqued the industry's "continued search for new fossil fuel reserves," reminding the executives that "the Paris Agreement clearly urged keeping most fossil fuels underground."[7] He called on the leaders to take the lead in accelerating the transition to clean energy.

A year later, he met the executives again, this time expressing greater urgency. Since their 2018 meeting, the alarming Intergovernmental Panel on Climate Change Special Report 1.5 (IPCC 1.5) had appeared, warning that humanity had about a decade to dramatically reduce greenhouse gases. Francis did not mince words, referring to a "climate emergency" for the first time and noting that "the ecological crisis, especially climate change, threatens the very future of the human family." [8]

"I beg your pardon, but I would like to emphasize this: they, our children and grandchildren, should not have to pay . . . the price of our irresponsibility. . . . Today's young people are saying, 'The future is ours,' and they are right!"[9]

"Dear friends, time is running out! Deliberations must go beyond mere exploration of what can be done, and concentrate on what needs to be done, starting today. . . . The climate crisis requires 'our decisive action, here and now.'. . . Today a radical energy transition is needed to save our common home."[10]

Today, we stand at the cusp of a new energy revolution: the shift to renewable energies—solar, wind, geothermal, and other

6. Pope Francis, "Address of His Holiness Pope Francis to Participants at the Meeting for Executives of the Main Companies in the Oil and Natural Gas Sectors, and Other Energy Related Businesses," Vatican City, June 9, 2018, www.vatican.va.

7. Pope Francis, "Address of His Holiness Pope Francis to Participants at the Meeting for Executives . . . Oil and Natural Gas Sectors."

8. Pope Francis, "Address . . . Energy Transition & Care of Our Common Home."

9. Pope Francis, "Address . . . Energy Transition & Care of Our Common Home."

10. Pope Francis, "Address . . . Energy Transition & Care of Our Common Home."

clean sources of power—and to smart technologies. The challenge is to do so rapidly and to secure the gains made by economies over the past two centuries while rejecting the pollution and environmental neglect of the industrial model of development.

DEGREES OF TROUBLE

The basics of the climate crisis are now widely understood: industrial societies have thickened the blanket of greenhouse gases that surround our planet and regulate its temperature. By burning fossil fuels, clearing forests, and raising food unsustainably, we shift carbon and methane from deposits underground, and from trees and soils, into the atmosphere, where they now insulate the planet to an excessive degree—or degrees. For our purposes, the highly complex issue of climate might be distilled to a question of one degree, two degrees, and more.

Human activities since the late nineteenth century, when fossil fuel burning began to tick up noticeably, have raised the average global temperature by about one degree Celsius. One degree is meaningful—it is a bigger and much faster change than human civilizations have experienced over their 11,000 years of development.[11] Indeed, the remarkable climate stability over these millennia has made possible the rise of civilizations, because climate stability allowed agriculture, a prerequisite for cities, to take root and flourish.[12] But humanity's relentless pursuit of unsustainable activities over the past two centuries has

11. Dr. Katharine Hayhoe, Texas Tech University, personal communication, August 17, 2020.

12. Michon Scott, "What's the Hottest Earth Has Been 'Lately?'" NOAA Climate.gov, September 17, 2014, https://www.climate.gov; Emily Sohn, "Climate Change and the Rise and Fall of Civilizations," NASA Global Climate Change, January 20, 2014, https://climate.nasa.gov.

caused greenhouse gases to accumulate in the atmosphere so that temperatures now lie at the outer edge of any warming our civilizations have ever known.

Early evidence of dangerous warming has already arrived with just one degree of temperature rise. Once-rare storms of ferocious energy and voluminous rainfall now occur regularly across our planet. Wildfires like the ones in Australia and California destroy entire towns and strip massive areas of trees and wildlife. Glaciers are melting worldwide, often threatening the summer water supplies of downstream cities. Droughts threaten water supplies and agricultural output in some regions. Species extinctions accelerate with climate change, oceans are rendered warmer and more acidic, and biodiversity is reduced. In addition, migrations of people from Syria into Europe, and from Central America toward the United States, have been linked to climate-exacerbated crop failures, possibly a harbinger of the tens to hundreds of millions of people who could be displaced, largely by sea-level rise, in the decades ahead.[13]

Less widely appreciated is the urgency of the climate crisis and the need for immediate action to restore climate stability. The 2015 Paris Agreement, signed by virtually all nations, calls for limiting temperature rise, compared to preindustrial times, to "well below" two degrees Celsius, and scientists have since advised that a 1.5-degree limit would be much less risky.[14] This cap on warming poses a huge challenge to the world's econo-

13. Kumari Rigaud et al., "Groundswell: Preparing for Internal Climate Migration," World Bank, Washington, DC, https://openknowledge. worldbank.org; Hayhoe, personal communication, August 17, 2020.

14. V. Masson-Delmotte et al., eds., "Summary for Policymakers," in *Global Warming of 1.5°C. An IPCC Special Report on the Impacts of Global Warming of 1.5°C above Pre-industrial Levels and Related Global Greenhouse Gas Emission Pathways, in the Context of Strengthening the Global Response to the Threat of Climate Change, Sustainable Development, and Efforts to Eradicate Poverty* (Geneva: IPCC, 2018).

mies, requiring a rapid transformation of the world's energy systems away from fossil fuels.

Donning Our Cap

A serious strategy for capping temperature rise at 1.5 degrees requires a major revamp of energy systems.[15] Industrial economies, after all, are built on carbon-rich coal, oil, and natural gas. A massive global mobilization is needed to achieve a series of increasingly challenging benchmarks:

- a peak in greenhouse gas emissions by 2020, then roughly
- a *halving* of those emissions by 2030, and roughly
- *a further halving each decade* to 2050.[16]

In addition to ending deforestation—another source of greenhouse gas emissions—this schedule means no new fossil anything: no new fossil-fuel power plants; no new oil wells; no new pipelines; no new drilling permits; and no new fossil-fuel financing. It also means massive decreases in fossil-fuel production.[17] This is what the 2015 Paris Agreement (and in 2019, Pope Francis) meant in asserting that fossil fuels should remain in the ground. This agenda does not suggest a casual, unhurried engagement. It requires concerted mobilization on the scale of the societal response to World War II.

An array of options must be tapped to replace fossil fuels and decarbonize the world's economies. Greater energy efficiency in everything from appliances to furnaces will be needed, and moderated consumption, rarely mentioned, is also required. And, of course, a key strategy for decarbonization is to replace

---

15. J. Falk et al., "Exponential Road Map: Scaling 36 Solutions to Halve Emissions by 2030," Future Earth (Stockholm: Future Earth, January 2020).

16. Falk et al., "Exponential Road Map."

17. https://350.org/keep-it-in-the-ground-just-how-much-exactly.

the energy foundation of our civilization with renewable sources: those sources of energy, such as wind and solar power, that are available perpetually and are clean in their production and use.

THE RENEWABLES OPTION

Renewable energy, once a niche power option, is becoming a mainstream solution for generating electricity. New power generating plants built in 2018 were more likely to be powered by wind, solar, and other clean energy installations than by fossil fuel and nuclear energy combined.[18] Still, renewables generated only about a quarter of the world's electricity in 2018, while the heating and cooling and transportation sectors feature relatively little renewable energy. So the energy sector overall has plenty of room for growth, and individual consumers, including parishes and parishioners, can help the renewables sector to advance. Options for accessing renewable energy are more numerous than ever, and they don't always involve bolting solar panels to one's roof.

---

2. Options for Accessing Renewable Energy

Utilities and contractors offer a number of strategies for shifting to renewable energy:

Pay for offsite renewable energy. Consumers can purchase renewable energy certificates (RECs), which verify that electricity was generated from renewable sources. REC electricity may not be the energy supplied to the consumer, but REC purchases help to support the renewables market. The electricity could cost more: in 2020, 100 percent renewable energy from Arcadia, a firm in Virginia, added 1.5 cents per kilowatt-hour to an

---

18. International Renewable Energy Agency (IRENA) "Renewable Capacity Highlights," March 31, 2019.

electricity bill—about 5 to 10 additional dollars per month for the average customer.[19]

Purchase solar services. Some consumers prefer to have renewable energy onsite but cannot afford a solar system. Many choose a power purchase agreement (PPA), a contract under which a solar services firm finances, installs, owns, and maintains the photovoltaic system on the buyer's property. The property owner agrees to buy electricity generated by the panels, often at low cost. In essence, the roof owner is "renting" the solar panels from the solar services provider.

Purchase solar panels. In this option, the property owner purchases the panels and is responsible for their installation and maintenance. The outlay is large, but savings on monthly energy bills are also large; and in many jurisdictions surplus energy can be sold to the utility, a financial bonus for owners.

Combined with increased efficiency of energy use and lowered consumption, and with an eye to reducing or eliminating fossil fuels in nonpower sectors such as transportation, residents and parishes can help reduce greenhouse gases, lower air pollution, and reduce pressure on our climate.

CLEAN ENERGY, CLEAN BUSINESS

The Catholic Energies (CE) model at the heart of the visionary Catholic Charities project in Washington is an inspiring example for advancing renewable energy among faith groups. CE helps Catholic parishes, schools, and other institutions to install solar panels, technologies for energy efficiency, or both, and finances the projects so that the institution does not have to raise any capital.[20] Its comprehensive technical services are complemented by a broad stewardship ethic inspired by *Lau-*

19. David (Arcadia representative), email to author, May 29, 2020.

20. Billy Ludt, "IGS Solar Installing 2-MW Solar Project for DC Catholic Charity," *Solar Power World*, July 10, 2019, www.igs.com.

dato Si'. The CCC sees CE as primarily an educational initiative that helps parishes, schools, retreat centers, and other facilities to demonstrate to users that the church cares about the environment and that these projects are part of what it means to live up to the demands of the Catholic faith.

It works like this. CE is a *project developer* that brings together various players to produce an unusual kind of energy deal. In the Washington, DC, case, Catholic Charities was CE's *client* and the host of the energy project. In other cases, the client is a Catholic school, hospital, or other institution. CE also brings in an *investor*, typically a renewable energy company, with experience in owning and operating renewable energy sites, and with access to capital to fund the project. The investor also owns and sells any renewable energy credits that come from the project,[21] and, with CE, hires the *contractor* to build the project.

CE aims to help institutions to save 10 percent or more on their electricity bills.[22] (For institutions pursuing environmental but not cost savings, the simple option is to use an energy supplier to purchase off-site renewable energy.) Cost savings are easier to achieve in areas with high energy bills among other factors, and good state and/or utility company incentives, among other factors. Indeed, in the Washington, DC, project, Catholic Charities will save 70 percent on its utility bill.[23] Where energy is less expensive, as in the hydropower-rich Pacific Northwest, the cost savings for clients are less.[24]

Misleh translates the financial savings into mission advance. In 2019, he told the online publication of an impact investing

21. Ludt, "IGS Solar."
22. Hannah Natanson, "A Field in D.C. Will Soon Be Home to 5,000 Solar Panels. It's All because of Local Catholic Groups—and a Message from the Pope," *Washington Post,* July 21, 2019.
23. Last, email to author, June 14, 2020.
24. Dan Last, discussion with author, October 10, 2019.

firm that savings from a switch to renewables could cover the salary of a youth minister, or perhaps two or three scholarships at a parish school. Efficiency upgrades also yield real savings. By swapping out lighting fixtures and bulbs to run LEDs, "the payback would probably be in two or three years," Misleh says, amounting to thousands of dollars in utility savings.[25] At the diocesan level, the savings can multiply. Diocesan investment in a sustainability director who could harvest energy savings at parishes and schools throughout a diocese could well pay for itself several times over.[26]

THE CATHOLIC ENERGIES DIFFERENCE

By demonstrating that important capital assets—the buildings at parishes, universities, hospitals, and other institutions—can become catalysts for a sustainability commitment, CE makes a concrete and growing contribution to addressing the climate crisis. But arguably as important, the program advances the idea that economic activity can be designed to serve the common good. Consider some of the organization's characteristic traits:

Values first. By taking a faith-directed approach, it is no surprise that CE has a strong values focus. "We are a witness to the wider community; they can see that Catholics are doing the right thing," is how Dan Misleh puts it.[27] Similarly, at the 2019 dedication of its CE solar project at Immaculate Conception Parish in Hampton, Virginia, Fr. John Grace

---

25. Sarah Brodsky, "Catholic Climate Covenant and Catholic Energies Take Action on Climate Change," Impactivate, https://www.impactinvestingexchange.com.

26. Daniel Misleh, interview with author, November 4, 2019.

27. Misleh, interview with author, November 4, 2019.

remarked that he was not merely interested in whether the parish could "save a few bucks. . . . I am interested in terms of the witness value of this parish, for a much larger world."[28]

Sufficiency. Organized as a nonprofit, CE takes a smaller-than-industry-standard developer's fee to fund its operation on a break-even basis. According to Dan Last, the group's chief operating officer, eschewing profit maximization and charging a low rate allows the firm to fund as many projects as possible.[29]

Ethical investment. The funding model is structured to attract impact investors, individuals or institutions seeking a social return on their investments, not just a financial one. The model also attracts donors interested in advancing ethical energy.

Multiple benefits. Misleh's vision for CE includes job training programs built around renewables installation, employment for homeless people, and the promotion of union laborers. CE already asks the institutions with whom they work if they have, and follow, a labor-union policy.[30] He also sees strong possibilities to practice solidarity. Some parishes and dioceses are wealthy, while others—say, in the inner city or on the U.S. southern border—are not; some face high energy costs and are strong candidates for CE partnership, while those with cheap energy are less obvious partners. Misleh asks, "Why not pool capital from all regions to invest in renewable energy, giving a decent average rate of return to all?" With a critical mass of projects and investments, Misleh claims, the dynamic of investments leading to energy savings and then to

28. https://soundcloud.com/icchampton/solar-panel-dedication, June 15, 2019.

29. Natanson, "A Field in D.C."

30. Misleh, interview with author, November 4, 2019.

more investment would feed itself, and the investment pool could become essentially a revolving fund.[31]

Strong stewardship. Catholic Energies has a knack for working idle assets. Instead of selling off land to pay for elderly members' health expenses, as some religious orders do, why not put idle assets such as roofs and land to work to generate revenue or reduce costs? In this way, an important asset can be retained and solve a financial problem rather than being liquidated.

Leavenings

Catholic Energies demonstrates a strong commitment to renewable energy, the foundation on which sustainable economies will be built. But its approach to energy development also stewards resources in a broad sense, thinking beyond energy to land use, the health of species, and social needs. And by imagining sharing the gains of renewable energy across dioceses, it leans into a solidarity that models a collaborative economics. In sum, CE offers a more environmentally and socially responsible way of being an energy firm.

It is easy to imagine the CE approach expanding, given the more than 250,000 places of worship in the United States.[32] And because such buildings typically have a strong public profile, their showcasing examples of solar leadership could help accelerate commitment to renewable energy across a community. To the extent that savings on energy bills are realized by faith communities, commitment to renewables could free up funds to advance a faith group's mission as well. Meanwhile,

---

31. Misleh, interview with author, November 4, 2019.

32. "All Places of Worship," Homeland Infrastructure, Foundation-Level Data, https://hifld-geoplatform.opendata.arcgis.com.

as community members commit to renewable energy at their homes, the environmental benefits of renewable energy could be multiplied rapidly. Through action across all of these dimensions, faith communities and their members would help to create a new energy foundation for our civilization—and, in the process, praise God through Brother Sun and Brother Wind.

Resources

Catholic Energies—the program of Catholic Climate Covenant that assists Catholic institutions to plan and execute renewable energy programs, https://www.catholicenergies.org.

Citizen's Climate Lobby—a nonpartisan group that advocates for national policies to address climate change, https://citizensclimatelobby.org.

Global Climate Change—NASA's climate page, which explains climate basics, https://climate.nasa.gov.

Green-e Certification Program—a project of Center for Resource Solutions, Green-e lists certified green power options for consumers and companies, https://www.green-e.org/certified-resources.

Interfaith Power and Light—organization that mobilizes people of faith to act on climate change, https://www.interfaithpowerandlight.org.

4

Food

In April 2010, Pleasant Hope Baptist Church in Baltimore celebrated Earth Day in perhaps the most grounded way possible. Equipped with shovels and hoes, Pastor Heber Brown and congregation members converted 1,500 square feet of the church's lawn into a vegetable garden, which became the group's living, ongoing linkage to the earth. The garden was also a nutritional lifeline, of course, generating more than 1,200 pounds of food, which the congregation donated to food-insecure families in the neighborhood.[1]

At the time, members could not have foreseen that their environmental effort would yield abundantly beyond its output of vegetables, spawning a social enterprise, a regional network of church-hosted gardens and farmers' markets, improved congregational health, stable markets for the region's African-American farmers, and a source of self-sufficiency and pride for this black Baptist church. Indeed, the Pleasant Hope experience of its garden and all that emerged from it suggests the potential for faith communities to move beyond the traditional (but still essential) work of feeding hungry individuals to creating a food system characterized by justice and resilience.

---

1. Edie Gross, "A Network of Black Farmers and Black Churches Delivers Fresh Food from Soil to Sanctuary," *Faith & Leadership*, May 28, 2019.

The budding potential of the church garden became clear in 2015, when police abuse of a young black man, Freddie Gray, sparked outrage in Baltimore. Soon after this event, the city was locked down, and some neighborhoods—many living under "food apartheid," without access to vegetables and other nutritional staples—were further cut off from sources of food. By this time, Pleasant Hope had earned a reputation as a center of food resilience, so Pastor Brown began fielding calls for help from neighborhoods that were low on food. The church garden's output was limited, of course, but Brown was resourceful. He called black farmers in the region and arranged to have produce sent to Pleasant Hope, where volunteers packaged the fruits and vegetables and delivered them to neighborhoods in need.

Brown's loaves-and-fishes success in expanding the food supply gave birth to a new, faith-based food provision system, the Black Church Food Security Network (BCFSN). The network is not a charity but a social enterprise for increasing resiliency. It promotes church-based vegetable gardens as well as Sunday farmers' markets at churches. It maintains a directory of at least twenty black farmers in eleven states—nearly all of whom use organic, regenerative, no-till, or other sustainable practices—to link them with black churches in their region and promote their businesses.[2] In 2020, it organized a Faith, Food, and Freedom summer campaign to promote local gardens, support black farmers, and practice emergency food storage.[3] Through these practices, BCFSN is a local expression of the global food sovereignty movement, which promotes local control of food production and distribution.

---

2. BCFSN, "Black Farmer Directory," https://blackchurchfoodsecurity. net.

3. BCFSN, "Faith Food, and Freedom Summer," https://blackchurch foodsecurity.net.

The church food network aligns beautifully with another of Pastor Brown's goals for his church: deepening a sense of pride and self-reliance in his congregation. Brown is inspired by black leaders since the 1960s who have connected food self-reliance with African-American freedom. Fannie Lou Hamer, a civil rights activist in the 1960s, turned to economic strategies to give black Americans a fair shake, founding the Freedom Farm Cooperative (FFC), a 640-acre enterprise in Mississippi owned and farmed collectively by black farmers. And Black Nationalist Albert Cleage Jr. helped to found Beulah Land Farm in South Carolina, the largest black-owned farm in the United States, as a symbol of black self-reliance. "Our self-determination begins with the ability to feed ourselves," Cleage is quoted as saying.[4] Pastor Brown has internalized this lesson; for him gardening is literally a political act.

Similarly, Pastor Brown is proud of traditional African agricultural practices that help black growers to heal soils while connecting them to African cultural roots. He is inspired by the approach of Leah Penniman of Soul Fire Farm in upstate New York, who teaches African farming practices that deepen topsoil, capture carbon from the atmosphere and sequester it in soils, and increase biodiversity.[5] Her educational programs on sustainable farming start with history, reviewing longstanding injustices to farmers of color that, for example, led to a decline in black ownership of U.S. farms from 14 percent in 1920 to just over 1 percent in 2017.[6] Penniman's historical approach includes important ecological components: for generations, enslaved

4. "The Beulah Land Farms Story—Mortgage Paid in Full October 2018," https://www.shrineoftheblackmadonna1.org.

5. "Farm Practices," Soul Fire Farm, http://www.soulfirefarm.org.

6. "Chapter V: Farm Statistics by Race, Nativity, and Sex of Farmer," https://www2.census.gov; the 1 percent figure is from National Agricultural Statistics Service, "Table 63. Selected Producer Characteristics by Race:

Americans passed along knowledge of African sustainable farming practices, and even African seeds. In the process, Penniman helps trainees to transform those environmental and cultural assets into sources of power and agency for African Americans today.[7]

The embrace of the environmental and political dimensions of food by Pastor Brown, Leah Penniman, and others is an important model for people of faith. How food is produced and distributed, where it is sold, who owns land and has access to credit—addressing these questions can broaden and deepen the traditional faith focus on feeding those who are hungry. Indeed, an enlarged understanding of food issues could help people of faith sow, till, and harvest a most valuable bumper crop: social justice on a healing planet.

Food and Agriculture Today

Global agriculture has an impressive record of output over the past half century, as the Green Revolution staved off predicted food shortages and mass hunger in the decades after 1970 but at a high cost over the long term. The achievements of industrial agriculture have taken such a toll on farm resources that, in combination with climate change, the future of the world's food systems is clouded. And as Pastor Brown's insights suggest, control of food production and distribution shapes the larger social and economic impact of the sector—for example, rural towns at the center of family farms are economically and socially distinct from towns surrounded by large corporate farms.

2017," *Census of Agriculture 2017* (Washington, DC: USDA, 2019), https://www.nass.usda.gov.

7. Kevon Paynter, "Black Farmers Reviving Their African Roots: 'We Are Feeding Our Liberation,'" *Yes!*, Spring 2018, www.yesmagazine.org.

Resource Use

Agriculture is a gigantic presence on our planet, dominating land use and water consumption, and requiring large amounts of fossil fuels. Farms and ranches cover about *half* of our planet's habitable area, for example, and account for about 70 percent of the water withdrawn for human activities. Beyond its sheer size, agriculture's impact relates to the way its most powerful practitioners work. Industrial agriculture is akin to an extractive industry; it depletes soil, groundwater, and fossil energy, much as copper is depleted from a mine over time. Over decades, the extractive approach to agriculture, which is characterized by large farms that are owned or influenced by corporations, ultimately undermines the basic units of our food system: land, water, and nutrients.

Farmland damage. Modern cultivation techniques, such as plowing, leave fields exposed to wind and water runoff that can carry away topsoil—the remarkably thin layer of earth that is the key to long-term farm productivity. Professor Duncan Cameron, professor of plant and soil biology at the University of Sheffield (UK), notes that on plowed fields erosion occurs up to one hundred times faster than it is regenerated through natural processes of soil breakdown over time. "This is catastrophic when you think that it takes about 500 years to form 2.5 centimeters" of topsoil under normal agricultural conditions, he observes.[8] The damage is widespread: studies in the 1990s and 2000s showed that 15 to 24 percent of the world's land suffers from erosion, salt buildup, and other forms of damage serious enough to reduce productivity.[9]

8. "Soil Loss: An Unfolding Global Disaster—Grantham Centre Briefing Note," Grantham Centre for Sustainable Futures, University of Sheffield, December 2, 2015, grantham.sheffield.ac.uk.

9. L. R. Oldeman et al., "World Map of the Status of Human-Induced

Overtapped water. As noted, agriculture is the thirstiest of human activities, accounting for 70 percent of the water appropriated by humans. Too often, it is overused. As discussed in chapter 5, groundwater (water from wells) is pumped faster than it is recharged by rainfall in major agricultural areas such as the Central Valley of California, the plains region of the United States, China, and India. Fields that depend on overpumped groundwater cannot sustain production indefinitely.

Wasted fertilizer. Fertilizer supplies nutrients to depleted soils, but chemical fertilizer used in industrial agriculture supplies three key ingredients (nitrogen, phosphorus, and potassium) without replenishing the organic matter and minerals that are also required for healthy soils—a nutrient regime akin to a hospitalized person who is fed intravenously. The loose nutrients in chemical fertilizer often run off into waterways and harm aquatic life. (By contrast, organic fertilizer does contain a healthy mix of ingredients, including organic matter that retains water and holds nutrients in place.) Moreover, phosphorus from phosphate rock is in limited supply and has no substitutes, but is not subject to conservation efforts.

In turn, the agricultural sector causes damage to the environment around it, especially to biodiversity, waterways, and the atmosphere.

Diminished biodiversity. Agriculture is a major contributor to biodiversity loss, through its conversion of natural habitats such as forests to simplified ecosystems, especially in the single

---

Soil Degradation: An Explanatory Note," Global Assessment of Soil Degradation (GLASOD), International Soil Reference and Information Centre, http://www.isric.org; and Z. G. Bai, "Proxy Global Assessment of Land Degradation," *Soil Use and Management* 24 (2008): 223–34, at http://www.geo.uzh.ch; similar findings are reported in United Nations Convention to Combat Desertification, *The Global Land Outlook*, Executive Summary, 1st ed. (Bonn: UNCCD, 2017).

crop cultivation patterns that dominate modern agriculture.[10] Biodiversity losses, in turn, are harmful to agriculture when they reduce nature's services to farmers, such as creating soil, providing pollination to plants, controlling pests and providing habitat to species important for food production.[11] But the biodiversity that supports agriculture, especially pollinators, natural enemies of pests, and soil organisms, are in decline as habitats are destroyed, overexploited, or polluted.[12]

Oceanic pollution. Meanwhile, industrial agricultural practices, including heavy use of chemical fertilizers, pesticides, and invasive tillage methods, are a serious source of pollution. For example, "dead zones" are now found along the world's coasts, areas where fertilizer runoff feeds micro-organisms that hoard oxygen in the water such that fish cannot survive. Some five hundred dead zones are now found in coastal areas worldwide, a tenfold increase from 1950.[13] They can be sizable: the dead zone in the Gulf of Mexico, caused by runoff from farms in the U.S. Midwest, was in 2019 about the size of New Jersey.[14]

Climate change. Agriculture (and associated deforestation) accounts for nearly a quarter of the world's greenhouse gas emissions.[15] These emissions come from carbon released when forests are cut down and soils are plowed, and from methane emissions

10. Nigel Dudley and Sasha Alexander, "Agriculture and Biodiversity: A Review," *Journal of Biodiversity* 18 (2017), 2–3, 45–49.

11. J. Bélanger and D. Pilling, eds., "The State of the World's Biodiversity for Food and Agriculture," FAO Commission on Genetic Resources for Food and Agriculture Assessments (Rome: FAO, 2019).

12. Bélanger and Pilling, eds., "The State of the World's Biodiversity."

13. Denise Breitburg et al., "Declining Oxygen in the Global Ocean and Coastal Waters," *Science* 359, no. 6371 (2018).

14. https://www.noaa.gov/media-release/large-dead-zone-measured-in-gulf-of-mexico.

15. P. Smith et al., "2014: Agriculture, Forestry and Other Land Use (AFOLU)," in *Climate Change 2014: Mitigation of Climate Change: Contribution of Working Group III to the Fifth Assessment Report of the*

from livestock. In turn, climate change is projected to reduce agricultural yields (food per acre) by 2 percent per decade—a shocking reversal of trends of the past half century—even as food demand is projected to increase by 14 percent per decade through 2050.[16] The new patterns could affect low-latitude (often developing) countries more negatively than high-latitude (often wealthy) ones.[17]

In sum, the extensive resource requirements of modern agriculture and the intensive way they are used in industrial-style production are harmful to agriculture itself and to other major Earth systems such as oceans and climate. These reasons alone suggest that industrial patterns of food production cannot be maintained and need to be replaced with sustainable forms of agriculture that focus on soil health. But the environmental toll of modern agriculture is only half of the challenge. Modern agriculture is often harmful to people as well.

SOCIAL AND ECONOMIC ISSUES

Because agriculture is part of a large socioeconomic system, it shapes societies in a variety of ways, many of them detrimental to human well-being:

Hunger and overweight. Food is abundant on our planet—so plentiful, in fact, that a large share is wasted, used to make etha-

Intergovernmental Panel on Climate Change, ed. O. Edenhofer et al. (Cambridge, UK, and New York: Cambridge University Press, 2014), 24.

16. IPCC, "Summary for Policymakers," in *Climate Change 2013: The Physical Science Basis. Contribution of Working Group I to the Fifth Assessment Report of the Intergovernmental Panel on Climate Change* (Cambridge, UK: Cambridge University Press, 2013), 3–32.

17. Cynthia Rosenzweig et al., "Assessing Agricultural Risks of Climate Change in the 21st Century in a Global Gridded Crop Model Intercomparison," *Proceedings of the National Academy of Sciences* 111, no. 9 (2014): 3268–73.

nol, fed to livestock, overconsumed by the two billion adults who are overweight or obese, and stored in reserves.[18] Yet 820 million people, about one in nine people globally, were hungry in 2018, the third consecutive year of increase after many years of decline.[19] And 11.1 percent of Americans were food insecure the same year, according to the U.S. Department of Agriculture.[20] Meanwhile, in 2016, nearly two in five adults globally—some two billion people—were overweight, according to the United Nations. The prevalence of obesity is increasing in all age groups and in all regions.[21]

Food waste. About a third of the world's food—and up to 40 percent in the United States—is wasted or lost every year.[22] This waste is not only a nutritional loss but a loss of the water, energy, and nutrient inputs used to produce the wasted food as well. Wastage represents unnecessary pollution, for example, in the runoff that creates dead zones along coasts worldwide and in the carbon pollution created by tractors and trucks that produce and distribute food. The United Nations reports that *if food waste were a country, it would be the world's third-largest emitter of greenhouse gases,* after China and the United States.[23] The upside, of course, is that cutting food waste could make a serious contribution to climate stabilization.

18. FAO, IFAD, UNICEF, WFP, and WHO, "The State of Food Security and Nutrition in the World: Safeguarding against Economic Slowdowns and Downturns" (Rome: FAO, 2019), www.wfp.org.

19. Hunger from FAO, IFAD, UNICEF, WFP and WHO, "The State of Food Security"; one out of nine is an author calculation based on hunger and on world population, at United States Census Bureau, July 11, 2018, https://www.census.gov/newsroom/stories/2018/world-population.html.

20. Economic Research Service, "Food Security and Nutrition Assistance," USDA, https://www.ers.usda.gov.

21. FAO, IFAD, UNICEF, WFP and WHO, "The State of Food Security."

22. "Food Waste FAQs," USDA, https://www.usda.gov.

23. "Food Wastage Footprint & Climate Change," http://www.fao.org.

Diet. Livestock products can be especially resource-intensive, requiring more water, energy, fertilizer, and land for their production than other foods. This is because livestock require double helpings of resources—first, in the inputs required to grow their feed, then in the inputs required to raise the animal itself. Thus, the grain used to produce a kilo of beef would feed many more people if they consumed it directly rather than in the form of livestock products.

Fuel. Finally, a large share of corn in the United States—40 percent—is used for ethanol. Sometimes this reality is framed as a "fuel vs. food" dilemma. But in a world of food surpluses, this is a mistaken framing. Instead, the more relevant moral issue may be whether land should be used for biofuel when other energy options are available, and when that land could be returned to a more natural state.

Making global agriculture sustainable requires reform of our patterns of food production and consumption. On the production side, this means embrace of agro-ecological solutions that prioritize soil health and work in greater harmony with natural processes. It means food sovereignty, so that decisions about what is produced and how, and what the food chain looks like, are not controlled by concentrated corporate power. For consumers, reform means greater retail and consumer consciousness of food. In both cases, people of faith have an important role to play.

Faith and Food

Food and hunger issues are long familiar to people of faith. Traditional faith activities around food including actions such as volunteering at a soup kitchen, participating in food drives, and food-centered hospitality are regular parts of outreach work across many faiths (see below, 1. Langar: Food as Hospitality and Gesture of Equality). Now some parishes are getting dirt under the fingernails by setting up their own vegetable gardens, as Pleasant Hope did, to feed those in need within the parish or to supply soup kitchens. A few creatively supplement parish harvests with output from home gardens[24] or invite parishioners to cultivate seedlings at home, then transplant them into the parish garden.[25] St. Mark's Catholic Community in Boise also allots forty small plots to refugee families for their own cultivation—a source of nutrition as well as a gesture of welcome to help them adjust to their new homeland.[26] In these ways, churches bring parishioners and their food ministries closer to the soil, while building community.

---

1. Langar: Food as Hospitality and Gesture of Equality

Sikh communities have a well-developed approach to using food for hospitality and community building. Sikh services are followed by langar, a communal meal shared equally by members and visitors alike. Partaking together of a full vegetarian meal, served identically to all, is a ritualistic way of demonstrating the oneness and equality of humanity. It also helps to strengthen the sense of community among members of the gurdwara, the Sikh place of worship and education that provides the langar.[27]

The langar tradition extends back to 1481 at the Golden Temple in Amritsar, India. Today, the langar at the Golden Temple is likely the world's largest no-charge feeding center, serving 75,000 to 100,000 meals each day.[28] A commonly cited estimate suggests that Sikhs serve 6 to 7 million meals per day

---

24. https://stjoeparish.org/parish-community-garden.

25. "Garden Ministry," St. Mark's Catholic Community, https://www.stmarksboise.org.

26. "Garden Ministry," St. Mark's Catholic Community.

27. "Langar: The Communal Meal," The Pluralism Project, Harvard University, http://pluralism.org.

28. Layla Eplett, "The Logistics of One of the Largest Langars," *Scientific American* 22, November 2016.

around the world.[29] Impressively, Sikhs extend this hospitality outside the gurdwara as well, to people on the street who need food.

Waste Not

Congregations and individuals looking for climate action that is simple and offers a quick payoff should commit to reducing food waste. The United Nations' Sustainable Development Goal 12.3 targets a 50-percent reduction in food waste at the retail and consumer levels by 2030. It has a strong upside—lower food bills and reduced climate impact and resource use—at the cost of little more than greater awareness in meal planning and shopping. If 40 percent of food in the United States is wasted, the greenhouse gas emissions associated with producing, processing, and shipping that food is also wasted. Eliminating food waste would thus be a meaningful reduction in greenhouse gases. Recovering a sense of food as sacred could help.

Religious leaders easily make the connection between faith teachings and food waste (see below, 2. Giving Expression to Faith Teachings on Waste). In November 2019, Pope Francis spoke to the World Food Program in support of their Stop the Waste initiative, making explicit the link between food waste and climate change and calling for lifestyle change that will eliminate waste, "properly valuing what Mother Earth gave us."[30]

---

2. Giving Expression to Faith Teachings on Waste

Faith groups make strong links between their teachings and waste reduction. For example, Hazon, a Jewish organization

---

29. "Sikh Temples Serving Up Free Food for All," BBC, October 4, 2018.

30. Pope Francis, "Message of His Holiness Pope Francis for the Opening of the Second Regular Session of the Executive Board of the World Food Programme," November 19, 2019, www.vatican.va.

that promotes sustainability, bases its food stewardship recommendations on the biblical principle of *bal tashchit,* "waste
avoidance," and on the teaching of the medieval scholar Mai-
monides that it is forbidden to "destroy articles of food."[31] They
suggest several actions to live out these teachings, including
undertaking a food-waste audit; educating about reducing food
waste, hosting an event to incorporate leftovers into meals, and
implementing at least one ongoing initiative to reduce food
waste. They also suggest diverting leftover food to local food
pantries, volunteering as gleaners at a local farm, and sending
leftovers home with staff or guests.

For more than a decade, Green Muslims has promoted a
green version of Ramadan, the month-long period of daytime
fasting that culminates each evening in an *iftar,* a meal to break
the day's fast. Often celebrated in community, the *iftar* can generate voluminous quantities of food. So Green Muslims encourages commitment to "leftar," a play on *iftar* that denotes the
use of leftover foods and nondisposable dishware to reduce
waste. Their "Tips for Promoting a Zero-Waste Leftar" notes
that the practice advances three goals consistent with Islamic
teaching: reduce waste, benefit the environment, and help the
poor, through donations of leftovers. It also fulfills the Qur'anic
teaching that Muslims should "eat and drink: but waste not by
excess, for Allah loveth not the wasters."[32]

Food waste in wealthy countries is primarily a problem of
retailers and consumers, but food is also left in farm fields. Consumers can help reduce waste at the farm level by volunteering
to glean, perhaps with the Society of St. Andrews. The society
coordinates gleanings to reduce field waste and to supply soup
kitchens with produce.[33]

---

31. https://seal.hazon.org/activity_category/f3-food-waste.
32. "Leftar Poster," https://www.greenmuslims.org/ramadan.
33. "2019 Impact Report: Building Community. Feeding and Nourishing
Those in the Greatest Need," Society of St. Andrew, https://endhunger.org.

Promoting Ethical Diets

Because livestock products have such a large environmental footprint, curtailing or eliminating their consumption can help to lower the resource footprint of one's diet. In 1990, Fr. John Dear published the booklet "Christianity and Vegetarianism: Pursuing the Nonviolence of Jesus," which is still useful today.[34] And the Christian Vegetarian Association (CVA), an international, nondenominational ministry that advocates for plant-based diets in the lives of Christians globally, uses a newsletter, educational resources, discussion groups, and other tools to educate people about the healthful, environmental, and animal-welfare benefits of plant-based eating.[35] For example, they offer a three-part curriculum for high schoolers and adults, called the Psalm 24 Project, which encourages discussion of humanity's duties to "God's earth, God's animals, and our God-given bodies."[36] And viewing vegetarian advocacy as "a form of Christian stewardship and discipleship," they also encourage members to spread the word about vegetarianism, in appropriate ways, at Christian gatherings.[37]

Congregations that are not ready to set a strict vegetarian policy still have options for reducing their environmental impact from meat. Because chicken is the least environmentally impactful meat, followed by pork and then beef, substituting chicken for beef amounts to a meaningful reduction in environ-

34. "Christianity and Vegetarianism: Pursuing the Nonviolence of Jesus," http://www.afa-online.org.
35. "Our Mission" web page of Christian Vegetarian Association, https://christianveg.org.
36. "Psalm 24 Project," web page of Christian Vegetarian Association, https://christianveg.org.
37. "How to Help," web page of Christian Vegetarian Association, https://christianveg.org.

mental impact from diet.[38] Congregations might also consider "default vegetarian" guidelines, a movement in the catering industry that could well be applied to congregational gatherings where food is served. The idea is to make plant-based offerings the norm, while offering people the option to choose meat. For example, a spaghetti dinner might have a meatless tomato sauce, to which individual participants could add meat if they desired. This strategy is inclusive of meat eaters, but still likely reduces the environmental impact and increases the healthfulness of a community meal. It also subtly shifts participants' understanding of what a "normal" meal is.[39]

Consumers can also impact the food system by being mindful of where our food originates. Catholic Rural Life (CRL) notes that it is important to keep local farmers on the land by buying their produce. If your town has a farmers' market, parishioners might be encouraged to use it. If not, a parish parking lot might be useful for setting one up; on Sunday mornings, farmers would find a ready market, and parishioners would have convenient access to fresh food. Alternatively, a church might purchase food from farmers, store it at the parish hall, and sell it to parishioners who pay a subscription. For low-income parishioners, the fee might be waived. A variant of this is community supported agriculture (CSA), in which residents or parishioners might purchase a "share" of a farmer's output early in the season, then receive a portion of the weekly harvest. The early season payment improves cash flow for farmers, and a parish delivery site simplifies logistics.

38. Gidon Eshel et al., "Land, Irrigation Water, Greenhouse Gas, and Reactive Nitrogen Burdens of Meat, Eggs, and Dairy Production in the United States," *Proceedings of the National Academy of Sciences* 111, no. 33 (2014): 11996–12001.

39. "Default Veg," https://defaultveg.com.

Deepening the Roots of Food Justice

A multitude of opportunities exists to fill out faith actions on food. Institutions such as Catholic Rural Life and the Unitarian Universalist Association have a number of ideas for broadening faith thinking on food issues, from both the production and consumption perspectives. Most Americans live in urban environments, have little exposure to farming and the food system, and may be unaware of justice issues in agriculture. So education on food and agriculture is important. CRL puts out a series of one-page fact sheets that can become bulletin inserts for parishioners or for advocacy when writing to elected officials. The fact sheets cover a wide range of issues, from the plight of farmworkers to conserving water and care for the land.[40] Unitarian Universalists offer a helpful resource as well.

---

3. The Many Dimensions of Food

More than a decade ago, Unitarian Universalists produced an excellent food resource entitled "Ethical Eating," which remains useful today for helping congregations to shape their approach to food and hunger issues. Over fifty pages it covers a comprehensive set of actions that could provide congregational food programming for years. Challenges examined include hunger, farmworker injustice, and trade issues. It also looks at solutions including fair trade, organics, and "slow food."[41]

In addition to its one-pagers, Catholic Rural Life offers a "Faith-Based Study Guide on Poverty and Hunger," which applies the "see, judge, act" method of reflection and action to food and agricultural issues. The method requires understanding the lived real-

---

40. "Fast Facts for a Just Food System," Catholic Rural Life, https://catholicrurallife.org.

41. "Ethical Eating: Food and Environmental Justice," Unitarian Universalist Association (Boston: UUA, April 2010), https://www.uua.org.

ity of farmers, farmworkers, food distribution systems, corporate actors, and other dimensions of the food system (seeing); using scriptural texts and church documents to assess those dimensions from a faith perspective (judging); and developing strategies to address injustices identified in the system (acting).

Although some of the material requires updating, the guide is useful in moving readers well beyond soup kitchens and food drives—essential as these are—to understanding the systemic problems in food today. For example, the "seeing" section explores hunger's roots in poverty rather than food scarcity, the shortcomings of free trade as an answer to hunger, and the difference that sustainable, local food systems can make. Other issues considered outside the guide by CRL include the position of refugees, the importance of water conservation, and the dignity of work in the food-processing industry.

Consumers have a role to play in creating a more just and sustainable food system as well because, as Catholic Rural Life states, "Eating Is an Ethical Act." Our work can start by recovering a sense of food as sacred. It is a sad irony that the bounty of American agriculture may have blinded us to the precious nature of food: cheap food is easily viewed as a mere commodity rather than a daily gift from God, through our bountiful Earth. So reclaiming the sacredness of food is important—in itself, but also because it helps us to think about what we eat, where our food originates, and how efficiently we harvest, process, and eat it.

LEAVENINGS

Creating food and agricultural projects with a concrete justice dimension and systems perspective offers an inspiring way to broaden faith communities' traditional charitable work of feeding the poor. Initiatives like the Black Church Food Security

Network multiply the impact of a faith community, create more resilient food security and food sovereignty regimes, and raise consciousness of the political economy of food. This, in turn, can increase advocacy on food issues and potentially affect national food policy. In these ways, a broadened approach to thinking about food and agriculture advances many precepts of Catholic Social Teaching, from solidarity and the dignity of the human person to care for God's creation, making an option for the poor, and promoting the dignity and rights of workers.

Because we all eat, we all have a fork in the food and agriculture systems that nourish us. Imagine if all parishes and congregations made food sovereignty, regenerative agriculture, and support for local farmers mainstays of members' consciousness around food, through concrete projects like church gardens and relationship building with farmers. Imagine further if all people of faith were conscious of reducing food waste and reducing the impact our consumption of food has on the climate, especially by eating lower on the food chain. From soil to sky, the impact would be profound.

RESOURCES

Black Church Food Security Network—a network of churches and farmers promoting food sovereignty and food security for African-Americans, https://blackchurchfoodsecurity.net.

Catholic Rural Life—organization that champions faith values among rural communities, https://catholicrurallife.org.

Christian Vegetarian Association—nonprofit that promotes vegetarianism among Christians, https://christianveg.org/default.htm.

Ethical Eating: Food and Environmental Justice—publication of Unitarian Universalists, https://www.uua.org/environment/eating.

5

Water

Father Thomas Loya had new neighbors on his mind when he purchased a ten-acre parcel in Homer Glen, Illinois, to become the site of Annunciation Byzantine Catholic Church. Residents bordering the property worried that the church's developmental footprint would worsen the parcel's long-standing flooding problem, and they vowed to oppose the church purchase.[1] Father Loya had quite the sales job ahead of him. But he also had quite the plan—a vision to restore much of the property to native prairie and wetland, with a goal of reclaiming the land's natural ecology. Ecological restoration, he explained to neighbors, would solve the seasonal flooding issue that had long afflicted the neighborhood.

The neighbors were skeptical, but Loya hired a consultant and got to work. He planted native grasses and flowers whose extensive root systems cleanse flowing water and eliminate runoff. Rain gardens help to channel water to underground cisterns for storage. A permeable pavement system allows water to percolate into soils rather than run off to storm sewers, thereby cleaning up a nearby detention basin and nurturing new vegetation that increases the ground's biodiversity. An old windmill runs

1. Fr. Thomas Loya, Annunciation Byzantine Catholic Church, Homer Glen, IL, interview with author, May 8, 2020.

an aerating pump that oxygenates a pond on the property, balancing pH levels against any chemical contaminants that might wash from offsite into the pond.[2] The result is "a church in a natural environment—a living land that grows with the people who care for it and love it," according to the parish website.[3]

Integrated into the restored landscape, now an expanse of waist-high grasses and a gurgling stream, are contemplation gardens featuring Byzantine icons or statues that invite reflection on Scripture or on nature itself. Paths linking the meditation sites extend to the neighborhoods that border the property and could one day connect to a broader system of nearby trails, encouraging community use. Indeed, Fr. Loya frames the parish's ecological restoration work as gifts to the community.[4]

Father Loya's ecological passion emerges from his Eastern Catholic spirituality. For him the parish grounds are "a vision for a new type of dialogue between people, their faith, and the Eden given to us from God."[5] Eastern Rite churches emphasize the sacramental and liturgical nature of human experience—sacramental in the sense that the material world is a gift and revelation of God, and liturgical meaning that these gifts are gratefully received and offered back to God.[6] Loya sees the restoration work as a concrete expression, through nature, of the liturgical, sacramental worldview.

So extensive and successful was the restoration effort that the church has won four local environmental awards in addition to a regional "Excellence in Conservation" award from Chicago Wilderness, a conservation organization in the four-state area

2. Loya, interview with author, May 8, 2020.

3. "Overall Vision," Annunciation Byzantine Catholic Church, http://byzantinecatholic.com/nature/overall-vision/.

4. Loya, interview with author, May 8, 2020.

5. "Overall Vision."

6. Loya, interview with author, May 8, 2020.

around Chicago.[7] Among those making nominations for the local awards: the neighbors who had initially objected to the church moving in! Loya observes that the parish "has solved a water problem and has become a community park, where people feel they can go. That's what we had hoped for. It's a joy to see that we no longer have a problem with water and a joy to see the neighbors using the property." This happened, he says, because "We look at nature . . . as a gift, as opportunity."[8]

The parish's ecological vision is not yet fully realized. The hope is to have a green roof someday—a roof with vegetation that will channel water down to the rain garden and, in conditions of overflow, into the underground cistern for recirculation. The green roof could also help to insulate the church, reducing its energy requirements and heating and cooling bills. He also envisions onsite renewable energy providing much of the parish's energy. The parish summarizes the legacy of its stewardship this way: "Annunciation Parish will be a place where the landscape is alive, plants will reproduce, and stewards will be taught to hear and understand the landscape."

The Annunciation experience is a useful parable for broadening our thinking about water stewardship. Too often, water conservation focuses on the faucet—that ordinary piece of hardware that marks where the planet's water meets our needs. For many, it's "where our water comes from." Certainly, end-use conservation is a critical piece of caring for water, as the discussion below demonstrates. But there is an important upstream world behind the tap—the rivers, lakes, and rainfall that supply our water—that is critical for ecological health and for meeting

---

7. Board of Trustees, "Board Meeting," Village of Homer Glen, Illinois, November 28, 2006, http://www.homerglenil.org/AgendaCenter/ViewFile/Minutes/_11282006-1228; Loya, interview with author, May 8, 2020.

8. Loya, interview with author, May 8, 2020.

human needs. Good water stewardship involves caring for this system across its entire course, from clouds to earthly use.

WATER, WATER, EVERYWHERE . . .

Our planet's water situation can be confusing. On the one hand, Earth is awash in water: three-quarters of the surface is covered in it; lakes and rivers, sometimes mammoth ones, are found on every inhabited continent. Indeed, our planet has 117 million lakes.[9] Earth is called the Blue Planet for a reason.

Yet water scarcity is real. Much of our planet's water is salty or locked in icecaps and glaciers. Liquid freshwater, the sweet resource so highly valued by humans and other species, amounts to less than 1 percent of all the water on the planet and is found in very short supply in some regions, especially arid ones.[10] In sum, our planet has plenty of water overall, but it is sometimes unavailable where and when it is needed.

In fact, half a billion people live in conditions of water scarcity, and 4 billion people—more than half of the global population—experience severe water scarcity for at least one month of the year.[11] The World Resources Institute estimates that seventeen countries, most in the Middle East and North Africa, are living with "extremely high" levels of water stress, meaning that farms, factories, and cities use 80 percent or more of the available supply of water each year.[12] Adapting to extreme scarcity,

9. Charles Verpoorter et al., "A Global Inventory of Lakes Based on High-Resolution Satellite Imagery," *Geophysical Research Letters*, August 12, 2014, https://www.researchgate.net.

10. USGS, Water Science School, "Where Is the Earth's Water?" USGS, https://www.usgs.gov.

11. Mesfin M. Mekonnen and Arjen Y. Hoekstra, "Four Billion People Facing Severe Water Scarcity," *Science Advances* 12 (February 2016), https://advances.sciencemag.org.

12. Rutger Willem Hofste, Paul Reig, and Leah Schleifer, "17 Countries,

as nations like Israel have done, is possible only to a point. The World Bank and United Nations have estimated that some 700 million people could be displaced by water scarcity by 2030.[13]

The problem is no longer hypothetical in a growing number of cities. In 2014, water in reservoirs supplying São Paulo, Brazil, dropped to just 5 percent of capacity, and residents were facing severe shortages.[14] In Cape Town, after years of drought and steadily ratcheted water restrictions, the mayor, in October 2017, issued an emergency plan that identified the projected arrival of "Day Zero" the following March, when critically low dam levels would trigger a shutoff of city water.[15] And in Chennai, India, a city of 11 million people, three of the city's main reservoirs ran dry in 2019; water had to be shipped in by truck and train.[16] As demand for water increases in many cities, including those in wealthy countries, scarcity scenarios like these could be replayed repeatedly.

But not necessarily. Scarcity is often created or worsened by unwise management practices—whether poor management of upstream supply or poor management of demand. In other words, scarcity does not always indicate physical shortage; cities

Home to One-Quarter of the World's Population, Face Extremely High Water Stress," World Resources Institute, August 6, 2019, https://www.wri.org.

13. UN Global Compact, "Making Every Drop Count: An Agenda for Water Action (2018)," CEO Water Mandate, https://ceowatermandate.org.

14. Suzanne Ozment and Rafael Feltran Barbieri, "Help for São Paulo's Complex Water Woes: Protect and Restore Forests," World Resources Institute blog, September 25, 2018, www.wri.org.

15. M. J. Booysen, M. Visser, and R. Burger, "Temporal Case Study of Household Behavioural Response to Cape Town's 'Day Zero' Using Smart Meter Data," *Water Research*, preprint, November 13, 2018.

16. Arati Kumar-Rao, "India's Water Crisis Could Be Helped by Better Building, Planning," *National Geographic,* July 15, 2019; Swati Gupta, "Indian Water Train Arrives with Desperately Needed Relief for Chennai," CNN, July 12, 2019.

may have more control over their supply of water than appears to be true at first glance. Often, water scarcity is created by a myopic "faucet-forward" consciousness that ignores potential scarcity solutions for water before it ever reaches a tap. As people of faith develop an expanded water awareness, understanding issues behind the tap becomes important. Consider, for example, these common drivers of scarcity in a water-supply system:

Neglected infrastructure. The story of São Paulo's water scarcity in 2015 involved a combination of drought, poorly maintained pipes, pipelines, and other infrastructure; and environmental mismanagement.[17] For example, forests surrounding São Paulo's main drinking-water system once filtered water and held water in soils. But more than three-quarters of this wooded land has been degraded, and water arriving to São Paulo must be treated to remove sediment—the filtering function that trees once did naturally and at no cost. In one analysis, the World Resources Institute has concluded that restoring 4,000 hectares of forests in the watershed could improve water quality by reducing the sediment load, at a net savings to the city.[18]

Pollution. Pollution can render precious water supplies unusable. A dramatic case is the contamination of drinking water with lead in Flint, Michigan, which led authorities to supply the largely African American residents with bottled water for years.[19] Despite the passage of the Clean Water Act of 1972, which mandated that the nation's waters become "fishable"

17. Suzanne Ozment, Rafael Feltran-Barbieri, Erin Gray, "Natural Infrastructure in Sao Paulo's Water System," World Resources Institute, September 2018, https://www.wri.org/publication/natural-infrastructure-sao-paulo.

18. "Natural Infrastructure."

19. Karen Pinchin, "The EPA Says Flint's Water is Safe—Scientists Aren't So Sure," *Frontline*, September 10, 2019.

and "swimmable" by the mid-1980s,[20] the National Water Quality Inventory report to Congress in 2017 noted that 55 percent of surveyed rivers and streams in the United States were unable to support fishing, swimming, or other uses designated for them by states.[21]

Climate change. The climate crisis is also an overarching source of water scarcity (as well as, paradoxically, flooding). Climate change is already intensifying droughts in the United States. This affects agriculture, industry, and household water supplies but also sectors such as energy, where hydropower, for example, needs robust river runs to function properly.[22] Even where total precipitation is unchanged, warmer temperatures may mean that mountain precipitation falls as rain rather than snow, thereby reducing mountain snowpack. In places like California, Peru, and northern India, mountain snowpack serves as a reservoir that melts gradually in the spring and summer, releasing vital water in dry seasons. These water supply issues are important to faith groups as a general matter of public policy; an ethic of care for creation suggests that advocacy is needed to care for upstream watersheds, city water infrastructure, and pollution reduction. More directly, some faith groups own extensive tracts of land—for example, at retreat centers or universities—whose proper management might contribute to higher water quality and stewardship downstream.[23]

Water scarcity can also be created by poor habits of water use. Here are two examples:

20. U.S. Environmental Protection Agency, "Statute and Regulations Addressing Impaired Waters and TMDLs," https://www.epa.gov.

21. U.S. Environmental Protection Agency, "National Water Quality Inventory: Report to Congress," August 2017, https://www.epa.gov.

22. U.S. Global Change Research Program, *Impacts, Risks, and Adaptation in the United States: Fourth National Climate Assessment*, vol. 2 (Washington, DC: USGCRP, 2018).

23. This topic is outlined in more detail in chapter 7 of this book.

Overpumping. Groundwater, an unseen but voluminous source of water in many regions, can be tapped indefinitely if stewarded well—if, over the long term, aquifers are pumped no faster than they are recharged by rainfall. But overpumping is draining an estimated 20 percent of the world's aquifers, many in highly productive agricultural areas such as the California Central Valley and High Plains of the United States, the North China Plain in China, and the Upper Ganges basin of India and Pakistan.[24] Overuse in these regions is a direct threat to food supply. For example, in the Central Valley of California, which provides a food supply for the United States,[25] eleven of fifteen monitored basins are critically overdrafted.[26]

Food choice. Animal products are particularly water-intensive; almost a third of the water consumed in agriculture globally is used in the production of livestock products (including the water used to grow feed for animals).[27] Animal products have a larger component of water than crops that supply the same nutritional value. The picture has important nuances as well: beef is more water-intensive than chicken or fish, and 20 times more water-intensive than nonmeat foods such as grains and starchy roots.[28] Also important is how animals are raised. Animals that graze consume less water than animals raised in feedlots. Thus, consuming meat with a smaller

24. United Nations Environment Programme, "A Glass Half Empty: Regions at Risk Due to Groundwater Depletion," 2012, https://na.unep.net.

25. "California's Central Valley," USGS, https://ca.water.usgs.gov.

26. Ellen Hanak et al., "Water and the Future of the San Joaquin Valley," Public Policy Institute of California (Sacramento: PPIC, February 2019), www.ppic.org.

27. Mesfin Mergia Mekonnen and Arjen Hoekstra, "A Global Assessment of the Water Footprint of Farm Animal Products," *Ecosystems* 15 (2012): 401–15.

28. Mekonnen and Hoekstra, "Global Assessment."

water footprint, or avoiding meat altogether, can save voluminous quantities of water.[29]

Because water is central to all economic activity and critical for human life, water scarcity, whether natural or created by
mismanagement, is a drag on development. The United Nations
notes that water "flows through and connects the 17 Sustainable Development Goals (SDGs)" given its central importance
to the economy, environment, and health, among other sectors.[30]
Indeed, where water is scarce, serious social and health problems quickly arise. UNESCO reports that more than a quarter of the world's population lacks access to safe drinking water
and that more than half lack access to proper sanitation.[31] The
health consequences can be dire: UNICEF says that six thousand children die each day because of water-related diseases.[32]
Even where scarcity does not produce death, the consequences
for development can still be dramatic, as seen in the water crises
in cities like São Paulo, Cape Town, and Chennai.

Faith Responses

Water is dear to people of faith as a symbol of purity, cleanli-
ness, and initiation, and as an ever-renewing source of life. Little
wonder, then, that when water is an issue, people of faith get
involved. Whether in shaping demand or caring about supply,
initiated by grassroots faith groups or high-level church leadership, water commands religious attention.

29. Arjen Y. Hoekstra, "The Hidden Water Resource Use behind Meat
and Dairy," *Animal Frontiers*, April 2012, http://www.waterfootprint.org.

30. Randall Hackley, "The World's Natural Aquifers at Risk," *Stockholm
Waterfront Magazine* 2, July 2018.

31. https://en.unesco.org/news/water-resources-essential-part-solution-
climate-change.

32. https://www.unicef.org/media/media_21423.html.

1. High-Level Leadership on Water

His All Holiness the Ecumenical Patriarch Bartholomew, spiritual leader of the world's 350 million Orthodox Christians, has a soft spot in his heart for water issues. Throughout his three-decade patriarchate, he has made environmental issues, and especially water issues, a key priority. Bartholomew has spearheaded a series of nine symposia on major bodies of water, from the Mediterranean, Adriatic, and Black Seas to the Danube, Mississippi, and Amazon Rivers, each featuring world-renowned specialists in environment, politics, and ethics.[33]

Bartholomew leveraged his connections with high-level political and religious leaders to elevate attention to water issues. Several of the symposia were organized in partnership with presidents of the European Commission Romano Prodi and José Manuel Barroso, and one included then–UN Secretary General Kofi Annan. On the Adriatic symposium, the stop in Venice featured a meeting between Bartholomew and Pope John Paul II, at which they jointly signed a document on environmental ethics.[34]

Bartholomew's leadership on water is an extension of his broader environmental interest. Since becoming patriarch in 1991, Bartholomew advanced the work started by his predecessor, Demetrios I, who designated September 1 a day for protection of the environment. Bartholomew also developed an Orthodox theology of the environment that included labeling environmental degradation a sin, a teaching that made global headlines, and advocating for repentance and inner transformation as useful responses to it.

Catholic leaders have often given water great attention because of its centrality to all life. Church representatives have been active in various World Water Forums since 2003, and

---

33. Alexander Maros, "The Ecological Theology of the Ecumenical Patriarch Bartholomew I," *International Journal of Orthodox Theology* 8, no. 1 (2017), 169ff.

34. Maros, "Ecological Theology."

Pope Francis devoted a section of *Laudato Si'* to water. Most recently, a publication of the Vatican's Dicastery for Integral Human Development on water, *Aqua fons vitae*, lays out Catholic thinking on water across many dimensions, including religious, cultural, economic, human rights, and spatial dimensions. The publication's various sections end with helpful recommendations for church institutions to become conscious of their approach to water, for example, by working to end polluting activities on church property.[35]

FAITH AND WATER ON THE GROUND

The 2018 water scare in Cape Town is a good example of a faith response to water. A drought had afflicted Cape Town for three years and had brought on various requirements for reducing water usage. By the fall of 2017, the city had pinpointed Day Zero, the moment in spring 2018 when city reservoir levels would fall to the point that water service to 3 million residents would be shut off. The result would be life altering: people would be required to line up at one of two hundred standpipes around the city to obtain a ration of water. In the end, Day Zero was avoided through conservation measures; water usage was cut almost in half, from 540 liters per household per day in January 2015 to 280 liters in January 2018.[36]

Religious communities responded to the crisis on multiple levels, from the individual to the watershed. Their immediate instinct was to care for those most vulnerable. Churches set up

---

35. Dicastery for Promoting Integral Human Development, "*Aqua fons vitae*: Orientations on Water—Symbol of the Cry of the Poor and the Cry of the Earth," (Vatican City: Dicastery for Promoting Integral Human Development, 2020).

36. Booysen, Visser, and Burger, "Temporal Case Study."

"Water Committees" to ensure that elderly and infirm individuals were matched with volunteers who would stand in line at the standpipes for their water ration.[37] But the Anglican community quickly moved beyond aid concerns to explore the justice implications of Day Zero, given the high levels of water consumption among wealthy white residents compared to those living in informal settlements. "We recognise that many citizens of Cape Town live day zero every day," wrote Rev. Rachel Mash, an Anglican minister. "They have to carry water every day. Going to the toilet involves a trip to filthy communal toilets with the risk of sexual harassment or rape."[38] Thus, the issue was framed as a justice issue that was greater than a temporary emergency and more than a mere glitch in supply.

Anglican parishes used the power of the Lenten season leading up to Day Zero to reflect on justice and on the reality of water scarcity. The Diocese of Cape Town published a thirty-two-page Lent Programme devoted to the water crisis. "We need to withdraw and reflect on our use of water," wrote Archbishop Thabo Makgoba. The reflection prompted by the programme was comprehensive; the booklet contained sections on sacredness, sustainability, sanitation, scarcity, and biodiversity. One reflection on scarcity reminded readers that food seemed to be in short supply in the story of Jesus feeding the five thousand, but that generosity solved the problem.[39] Other reflections framed water as a human right. "For us water is not a commodity to be

37. https://blog.arocha.org/en/countdown-to-day-zero-the-cape-town-water-crisis-and-what-it-tells-us/.

38. Rachel Mash, "What Are the Solutions for Cities Facing Water Shortages?," January 30, 2020, http://www.greenanglicans.org.

39. Karl Groepe, "A Theological Reflection On Scarcity," in Diocese of Cape Town, "Water (In)Justice: 2018 Lent Programme," www.green anglicans.org.

sold and bought. It is a fundamental human right which must be shared equitably. . . . Water is sacred. Water is life."[40]

Anglicans also made water education a priority, partly by setting a new tone and attitude toward the resource. Parishioners should see themselves as protectors of water, as people who conserve water. "We must fall in love with the joy of water," Rev. Mash wrote. But they also focused on the political economy of water, urging the faithful to learn the water footprint of their food and clothing, the role that water plays in energy supply (for example, the role of water in coal mining and fracking),[41] and other dimensions of water in making modern lifestyles possible.

Finally, people of faith were active in curbing consumption by becoming conservation conscious and participating in a 150,000-person "water-shedding" Facebook page.[42] They also worked to shore up supplies. The Anglican Church of Southern Africa called on parishes to install water tanks,[43] and after Day Zero citizens continued to be active in the "behind the faucet" water supply, cleaning rivers and protecting wetlands and water sources.[44]

LEAVENINGS

In much of the world, water is taken for granted, so abundant and easily accessed is this vital resource. But congregational efforts to amplify members' understanding of water from cloud

40. Mash, "What Are the Solutions?"
41. Mash, "What Are the Solutions?"
42. Mash, "What Are the Solutions?"
43. "The Anglican Church of Southern Africa Calls for Parishes to Install Water Tanks," Green Anglicans, September 27, 2019, www.greenanglicans. org.
44. Mash, "What Are the Solutions?"

to watershed to faucet can help to develop an appreciation for the integral importance of water to all of life. Father Loya's restoration of native wetlands, and the flourishing of species it nurtured, created a consciousness of water as gift, not merely as a resource. It also suggested the shortcomings of thinking about water as purely an engineering problem, given the role of the restored land in solving a long-standing flooding challenge. Furthermore, it showed that restoring land to the wild could contribute to faith development and worship, through the location of prayer stations on the restored land. Meanwhile, people of faith in Cape Town skillfully made the link between water use and justice.

Suppose all congregations examined their assumptions and understanding of the water they use. Suppose they traced their water back to its source and tallied the other creatures, human and nonhuman, in their neighborhood and region that depend on the same water, asking whether each can access the supply it needs. Suppose they studied how their use might be excessive, and how they might be polluting the supply. Suppose they analyzed who gets water and on what terms. Such an expanded worldview would surely open their consciousness to a fuller understanding of the gift of water in their lives. Expanded across the nation's congregations, such a consciousness would create an entirely new way of interacting with water and the ecosystems that water supports.

Resources

Dicastery for Promoting Integral Human Development, "*Aqua fons vitae*: Orientations on Water—Symbol of the Cry of the Poor and the Cry of the Earth" (Vatican City: Dicastery for Promoting Integral Human Development, 2020).

Diocese of Cape Town, "Water (In)Justice," Lent Programme, http://www.greenanglicans.org.

Water Footprint Calculator—helps individuals to measure their water footprint, based on direct and indirect water use, https://www.watercalculator.org/wfc2/complete/.

World Resources Institute—globally oriented research group focused on resource use, https://www.wri.org/our-work/topics/water.

6

Land

Leaders worldwide learned a critical lesson through the COVID-19 pandemic of 2020: unprepared nations pay dearly, in loss of life, human suffering, and economic costs and setbacks. In the future, those humbled leaders, especially in poor countries with minimal health infrastructure, could find help in preventing or managing future outbreaks from an unexpected quarter: faith communities. Molly Burhans, a young cartographer in New Haven and founder of the mapping firm GoodLands, sees immense potential in charting the lands and facilities owned by Catholic dioceses, religious orders, and other entities—then infusing the maps with environmental, social, and various health data. The resulting data-rich maps could guide critical decision making around the potential or actual outbreak of infectious disease.

For example, a map of dioceses in central Africa, overlaid with patterns of deforestation, which can spur the spread of infectious disease, might identify settlements at risk of an outbreak and prompt an appropriate preventive response. Overlay the map again with health clinics in the region, many run by faith groups, and the building blocks for a response strategy emerge. For Burhans, the potential of data mapping is huge. "COVID-19 highlights more than ever the need for expansion of Catholic environmental programs around the world," she explains. Environmental programs need to be "as serious a ministry as Catholic health care, and an extension of the ministry."[1]

Burhans's vision extends beyond health issues; data of many kinds can be married to maps to yield a diverse set of insights. For example, ecclesial jurisdictions from parishes and dioceses to provinces of religious orders can be analyzed, using different datasets, to reveal:

- tree cover, and populations of amphibians, birds, and mammals
- changes in growing season, carbon footprint, and hurricane data
- GDP, access to electricity, prevalence of malnutrition, estimated future GDP with climate change factored in, and agricultural land
- habitat connectivity, "green infrastructure," projected sea-level rise, heat waves, and migration patterns
- radio stations and other communications infrastructure
- hospitals, orphanages, and schools.

Burhans's key insight is that Catholic landholdings are extensive enough across churches, monasteries, orphanages, retreat centers, hospitals, seminaries, administrative centers, clinics, and schools that skilled management of them can contribute to meaningful environmental healing—and to advancing the church's social mission. But as a decentralized institution, the church does not typically see its landholdings from a broad perspective, including patterns of land use and the relationship between church holdings and neighboring lands. Mapping helps leaders to see the big picture.

According to Burhans, a global database of church lands

---

1. Colleen Dulle, "How Data Mapping Can Help the Vatican Fight COVID-19," *Inside the Vatican* (podcast), April 18, 2020, www.americamagazine.org.

could power "an implementation strategy for *Laudato Si'* " that will help build a just and sustainable world by identifying areas of social and ecological need and informing strategies to address them.[2] "Mapping is the matrix where Catholic Social Teaching comes to life," she says, noting that, for example, environmental data can be important for the relief and development work of Catholic Relief Services.[3] Furthermore, Burhans sees investment in mapping as offering important financial returns. The better land is managed, she observes, the more church and diocesan funds can be devoted to ministries.

GoodLands has analyzed the ecosystem services of more than 30,000 Catholic-owned properties in the United States,[4] helped the Vincentian order understand the ecological value of its East Coast properties, and analyzed the importance of green infrastructure (trees, streams, and other natural elements that provide ecosystem services such as water purification) on properties relevant to the U.S. Conference of Catholic Bishops.[5] In this work, GoodLands analyzes dozens of attributes, from soil health and quality to core habitat, extent of wetlands, and landscape connectivity.[6] If the bishops adopt a green infrastructure strategy, Catholic entities will be positioned to help their communities preserve and connect open areas, watersheds, wildlife habitats, and other critical spaces across large expanses of land. Burhans imagines such work scaling up to become a Catholic sustainability and conservation network that is as large and

2. "Vision: Mapping to a Brighter Future," GoodLands, https://good-lands.org; "Bringing Digital Transformation to the Catholic Church," *ARC News*, Winter 2019, www.esri.com.

3. Molly Burhans, discussion with author, February 7, 2020.

4. Timothy Schuler, "Mapping One of the World's Largest Landowners," *Curbed*, https://www.curbed.com.

5. "Project Highlight: USCCB Green Infrastructure Strategy," GoodLands, https://good-lands.org.

6. "Project Highlight."

robust as global Catholic networks in health care and education. "I think that's the challenge."[7]

Burhans is offering the church a new way of seeing, as a complement to St. Francis's sensual and heartfelt intimacy with nature. That intimacy teaches us to appreciate the rich reds and yellows of a tulip, the sun's warmth on our beached bodies, the lyrical gurgling of a stream in the woods. Data-rich mapping helps us to see in a new way by revealing nature at scale. Both are needed: internalizing the contours of the creation we have inherited, through heart *and* head, can elevate the environment to its rightful place in the work of people of faith.

A Weakening Fabric

The natural world might be likened to an oriental carpet, richly woven, with a multitude of interlaced threads telling a wonderfully complex story in lush color. Nature is a system of astounding intricacy that governs every square centimeter of the planet, at every moment and the next, generating oxygen, purifying water, and setting an on-time release of spring's first buds, to name a few items from a long to-do list. It is an extraordinary system that surely processes more transactions each microsecond, by orders of magnitude, than the world's stock exchanges do in a year. We witness only the tiniest fraction of these ongoing miracles, but there they are, unfolding in and around us, day in and day out.

But today this divine handiwork is damaged, the threads fraying, the transactions fewer and less robust, the whole weaker and less resilient in the face of shocks. Biodiversity loss may be the most underappreciated of the suite of sustainability chal-

---

7. https://www.curbed.com/2017/10/18/16483194/catholic-church-gis-goodlands-esri-molly-burhans.

lenges facing the planet and its people. It is one of the most consequential ways that we do not know nature. But it is evident in biological indicators such as extinction and the loss of nature's services—trends that are caused largely by human activities.

Extinctions are a regular part of biological life, as changing environments and genetic mutations reshuffle the cast of players in the never-ending creativity that defines our living planet. Extinction is ongoing. But mass extinction is a different matter entirely; only five have occurred in our planet's long history, most recently when dinosaurs and myriad other species disappeared 65 million years ago. Now we have entered Earth's sixth mass-extinction event—this one clearly caused by human beings. Extinctions are occurring "tens to hundreds of times" faster than the average of the past 10 million years, and extinctions are accelerating.[8] The International Union for the Conservation of Nature, a leading conservation organization, documents a massive potential thinning of the natural world: 25 percent of mammal species, 14 percent of bird species, and 41 percent of amphibian species are now threatened with extinction.[9]

As our ark loses species, the remaining populations are thinning. The Living Planet Index (LPI), which National Geographic describes as "a biologist's 'stock market index'"[10] of animal abundance, monitors thousands of population sets of more than four thousand mammals, birds, fish, reptiles, and

8. IPBES, "Summary for Policymakers of the Global Assessment Report on Biodiversity and Ecosystem Services of the Intergovernmental Science-Policy Platform on Biodiversity and Ecosystem Services" (Bonn: IPBES Secretariat, 2019), www.ipbes.net.

9. International Union for the Conservation of Nature (IUCN), "Table 1: Numbers of Threatened Species by Major Groups of Organisms (1996–2018)," IUCN Red List, http://cmsdocs.s3.amazonaws.com.

10. Elizabeth Anne Brown, "Widely Misinterpreted Report Still Shows Catastrophic Animal Decline," *National Geographic*, November 1, 2018.

amphibians.[11] The 2020 index found that over forty-six years, the population of these sets, taken together, had declined by 68 percent. Think about that: *the total population of monitored vertebrates fell by more than two-thirds in less than half a century.*[12] The geographic range of remaining species has shrunk as well. Nearly half of 177 mammal species surveyed for a 2017 study lost more than 80 percent of their geographic range between 1900 and 2015.[13] Little wonder that authors of the *Living Planet Report* conclude that "nature and biodiversity are disappearing at an alarming rate,"[14] while the authors of the range report describe the ongoing loss as a "biological annihilation."[15]

Many other indicators are consistent with findings of biological impoverishment. A 2019 study using satellite data found that vegetation that had been expanding globally in the 1980s and 1990s has stopped, likely because climate change is drying the atmosphere and limiting plant growth.[16] If the climate explanation holds, a continued decline in vegetation is projected as the planet continues to warm. Similarly, a famous study by citizen-scientists in Germany in 2017 found that in just twenty-seven years, the abundance of flying insects in German nature reserves

11. M. Grooten and R. E. A. Almond, eds., *Living Planet Report—2018: Aiming Higher* (Gland, Switzerland: World Wildlife Fund, 2018), 37.

12. R. E. A. Almond, M. Grooten, and T. Petersen, eds., *Living Planet Report—2020: Bending the Curve of Biodiversity Loss* (Gland, Switzerland: WWF International, 2020), 16.

13. Gerardo Ceballos, Paul R. Ehrlich, and Rodolfo Dirzo, "Biological Annihilation via the Ongoing Sixth Mass Extinction Signaled by Vertebrate Population Losses and Declines," *Proceedings of the National Academy of Sciences* 114, no. 30 (2017): E6089–96.

14. Grooten and Almond, eds., *Living Planet Report—2018.*

15. Ceballos, Ehrlich, and Dirzo, "Biological Annihilation."

16. Wenping Yuan et al., "Increased Atmospheric Vapor Pressure Deficit Reduces Global Vegetation Growth," *Science Advances,* August 14, 2019, advances.sciencemag.org.

had fallen by three quarters.[17] Two years later, professional scientists largely confirmed the findings in what some have come to call the "insect apocalypse."[18]

Biological impoverishment is not just a question of species counts. Nature supplies a vast range of services that meet the needs of humans and our many kin, from pollination of plants by bees, to water filtration in wetlands, to erosion prevention provided by tree roots.[19] Often overlooked in the public mind, these services are actually critical inputs to modern economies (see below, 1. Mother Nature Knows Best). Ecosystem services globally were valued in 2014 at an estimated $125 *trillion*.[20] But as ecosystems degrade, nature's services are lost or degraded as well, typically with economic impact. A 2019 global biodiversity assessment reported that land degradation has reduced productivity over nearly a quarter of the world's land area, and that hundreds of billions of dollars of crop production is at risk each year because of pollinator loss.[21]

---

1. Mother Nature Knows Best

The people of New York City understand the importance of ecosystem services. In the 1990s, the city faced a choice: spend $10 billion on a massive water filtration plant or invest one-tenth of that amount to maintain the biological health of the upstream region that supplies city taps. It chose conser-

---

17. Caspar Hallmann et al., "More Than 75 Percent Decline over 27 Years in Total Flying Insect Biomass in Protected Areas," *PLOS ONE*, October 18, 2017, journals.plos.org.

18. Sebastian Seibold et al., "Arthropod Decline in Grasslands and Forests Is Associated with Landscape-Level Drivers," *Nature*, October 30, 2019, www.nature.com.

19. The Economics and Ecosystems of Biodiversity, "Ecosystem Services," TEEB, http://www.teebweb.org.

20. Robert Costanza et al., "Changes in the Global Value of Ecosystem Services," *Global Environmental Change* 26 (2014): 152–58.

21. IPBES, "Summary for Policymakers."

vation over construction, buying land upstream to prevent development and the resulting pollution, reducing runoff from upstream farms, and ensuring that wastewater treatment plants in its watershed emit clean water.[22] By protecting the watershed's ability to supply clean water, New York saved enormous sums, protected the upstream environment, and safeguarded its reputation as the city with "the champagne of drinking water."[23]

Human activities drive the degradation of the natural world: we cut forests for farmland, convert wildland to urban use, overfish the oceans, dump waste into rivers and oceans, overfertilize agricultural land, and emit greenhouse gases, each of which is harmful to ecosystems and their inhabitants.[24] The aggregate environmental impact is surprisingly large; human activities claim between 25 and 40 percent of the planet's terrestrial primary productivity, a measure of the biological output from our planet's land and an indication of the extent of human domination of the environment.[25] When the human footprint is so large, many other species must fight to survive.[26]

Despite humanity's growing understanding of its damage to the natural world, corrective action is often not taken seriously.

22. Emily Lloyd and Michael Principe, "2006 Watershed Protection Program Summary and Assessment" (New York: Department of Environmental Protection, 2006).

23. Winnie Hu, "A Billion-Dollar Investment in New York's Water," *New York Times*, January 18, 2018.

24. Millennium Ecosystem Assessment, "Ecosystems and Human Well-Being" (Washington, DC: Island Press, 2005).

25. Yadvinder Malhi, "The Concept of the Anthropocene," *Annual Review of Environment and Resources*, September 11, 2017, 85, www.annualreviews.org.

26. Netherlands Environmental Assessment Agency (PBL), "Rethinking Global Biodiversity Strategies: Exploring Structural Changes in Production and Consumption to Reduce Biodiversity Loss" (The Hague: PBL, 2010), 38, www.pbl.nl.

Parties to the internationally agreed Convention on Biological Diversity in 2010 set up twenty targets to be met by 2020, ranging from halting overfishing and controlling invasive species to reducing the rate of deforestation. Not only were most of the goals not met by 2020, but because biodiversity health is integral more broadly to development, failure to meet the Aichi Biodiversity Targets is a drag on progress toward 80 percent of the targets of the UN's Sustainable Development Goals related to poverty, hunger, health, water, cities, climate, oceans, and land.[27] By neglecting the health of the planet that supports us and is our home, the human family risks the well-being of humanity as well.

FAITH CONTRIBUTIONS

Given the declining health of much of the natural world, what role might faith groups play in healing our planet? The world's faiths have a set of unique religious resources, including religious rituals, that are sometimes wielded in inspiring ways on behalf of biodiversity conservation. The potential for greater involvement is huge.

---

2. Ritual as a Tool for Environmental Protection

In Southeast Asia, where deforestation is a decades-long problem, Buddhist "ecology monks," in the late 1980s, began to step up to address the suffering brought on by forest clearing. For the monks, fighting forest clearing was a way of tackling its root causes: greed, ignorance, and hatred.[28] Among the initiatives adopted by the monks is the practice of "ordaining" a tree as one would a monk, with the same prayers, passages from the Pali Canon, and even dress—the tree is wrapped in a saffron robe. Typically a large tree is chosen as a stand-in for all

---

27. IPBES, "Summary for Policymakers."
28. Susan Darlington, "The Ordination of a Tree: The Buddhist Ecology Movement in Thailand," *Ethnology* 37, no. 1 (1998): 1–15.

the trees in the forest, with the goal of giving the forest a sacred character and protecting it from destruction. Tree ordination for Buddhists started in Thailand but has been practiced as well in Cambodia, Vietnam, and Sri Lanka and is credited with helping to spur conservation action in the region.[29]

A 2014 Swedish study found that the majority of areas important for biodiversity are found in countries dominated by Christianity.[30] In particular, they found the biodiversity–religion overlap to be especially strong in Latin America, with extensive biodiversity richness in predominantly Catholic countries. One of the co-authors, Hugh Possingham of the University of Queensland, observed that "Roman Catholics, per capita, have the greatest potential to preserve biological diversity where they live,"[31] suggesting a particular responsibility for Catholics. Religious and biodiversity overlap was also strong in areas that are predominantly populated by Buddhists, such as Southeast Asia; Hindus, on the Indian subcontinent; and Muslims, in Asia Minor and parts of North and Central Africa.[32]

An important multifaith effort on behalf of the natural environment is the Interfaith Rainforest Initiative (IRI), which advocates for the conservation of forests and the protection of their indigenous guardians. Founded in 2017, IRI brings together Christian, Muslim, Jewish, Buddhist, Hindu, and Taoist religious leaders, together with indigenous peoples from

29. August Rick, "To Protect the Environment, Buddhist Monks are Ordaining Trees," *Sojourners*, October 11, 2018, sojo.net.

30. Grzegorz Mikusiński, Hugh P. Possingham, and Malgorzata Blicharska, "Biodiversity Priority Areas and Religions—A Global Analysis of Spatial Overlap," *Oryx* 48, no. 1 (2014): 17–22.

31. Mikusiński, Possingham, and Blicharska, "Biodiversity Priority Areas."

32. Mikusiński, Possingham, and Blicharska, "Biodiversity Priority Areas."

nations that are home to major rainforests, to bring the power of moral clarity to international efforts to protect tropical forests. As part of its awareness-raising work, IRI produces a series of faith-specific tool kits and country briefs on tropical deforestation, a resource guide on rainforest protection, and a primer on forests and pandemics. It also works to mobilize action and influence policy.

IRI's work is critical. Despite agreements among governments, corporations, and NGOs to halt tropical deforestation over the past decade, the practice continues in major forested areas in Asia, Africa, and Latin America. The area of forests lost to deforestation since 2010 is about the size of the United Kingdom, France, and Germany combined. The meaning of the loss is hard to overstate: tropical forests store about half of the carbon found in vegetation, so deforestation reduces a critical carbon warehouse at a time when carbon absorption is more critical than ever. Tropical forests are also rich in species diversity, and they provide homes and livelihoods for millions of people, including indigenous people whose knowledge of the forests is key to their sustainable management. The expectation is that IRI will raise consciousness and advocacy for rainforests enough to make a critical difference in their conservation, just as individual faiths are doing increasingly.

---

3. Wielding Moral Authority on Behalf of Nature

In 2014, the government of Indonesia established the Global Tiger Recovery Program to double the population of endangered tigers and to protect more than a million hectares of tiger habitat. Program officials in the majority-Muslim country collaborated with Islamic leaders to raise awareness of the need to protect tigers. Indonesia's Islamic council of scholars, the Majelis Ulama Indonesia (MUI), supported the effort, issuing a "biodiversity fatwa," or edict—the first such fatwa ever to be issued. It laid out Islamic principles and teachings related to conservation, and prohibited the poaching and trading of tigers and other threatened species.

Officials of the Alliance of Religions and Conservation regard the measure as a strong signal linking species protection with the faith and religious duty of Muslims. The measure, and follow-on training, appear to have been impactful. The share of trainees who believed that the Qur'an teaches the importance of nature and that humans have an obligation to protect it grew from 50 percent before the training to 96 percent after it.[33]

If institutions might know nature and love creation through mapping, as GoodLands suggests, how can individual Catholics contribute to conservation? Here, the Saint Kateri Conservation Center in New York State is a helpful resource. It is named for Kateri Tekakwitha, the first female indigenous Catholic saint in North America, who was canonized in 2012. She is celebrated as a bridge between indigenous and nonindigenous peoples of the Americas and as a link among people, creation, and God.[34] The center was founded in 2000 to deepen Catholic faith through engagement with and conservation of nature. It offers retreats, a library of faith-related conservation materials, and innovative programs to help Catholics engage the natural environment directly.

One of these hands-on programs is the Saint Kateri Habitat Program, which encourages Catholics to set up conservation areas in yards, gardens, and schools, and where possible, on larger expanses of farms, forests, rivers, and wetlands. The idea is to help people honor God by increasing their love for nature. The program is open to individuals, parishes, schools, religious

33. Fachruddin Majeri Mangunjaya et al., "Protecting Tigers with a Fatwa: Lesson Learn Faith Base Approach for Conservation," *Asian Journal of Conservation Biology* 7, no. 1 (2018): 78–81.

34. "Saint Kateri Tekakwitha," Saint Kateri Conservation Center, https://www.kateri.org/our-patron-saint/.

orders, landowners, and others—anyone with a patch of land, including apartment dwellers with potted plants on a balcony. Participants agree to provide three straightforward biodiversity elements for their habitat, such as space for wildlife or for native wildflowers, along with a religious dimension, such as a cross or statue of Mary or St. Francis.

In 2020, the center listed 68 habitats in the United States. Kat Hoenke, the volunteer program director at the center, observes that the potential for growth is huge: with the program's simple criteria for participation, virtually every one of the nearly 21,000 parishes, pastoral centers, and missions in the United States, and every Catholic home, could host a Saint Kateri Habitat.[35] Such a large-scale faith and conservation presence is already a reality in other cultures.

---

4. Sacred Space as Protected Space

Forest cover in Ethiopia has fallen from nearly half the country a century ago to only 5 percent today.[36] The remaining forested area in the northern highlands of Ethiopia often consists of a string of small fragments of three to three hundred acres, each with an Ethiopian Orthodox church at its center.[37] Ethiopian forest ecologist and church member Alemayehu Wassie Eshete explains the sacred forests: "In Ethiopian Orthodox teaching, a church—to be a church—should be enveloped by a forest. It should resemble the Garden of Eden."[38] Traditional ecological knowledge, coupled with the reverence members

---

35. USCCB, "Parishes and Laity," USCCB, http://www.usccb.org.

36. Allison Abbott, "Biodiversity Thrives in Ethiopia's Church Forests," *Nature* 565, January 29, 2019, 548.

37. David K. Goodin, Alemayehu Wassie, and Margaret Lowman, "The Ethiopian Orthodox Tewahedo Church Forests and Economic Development," *Journal of Religion and Society* 21 (2019).

38. Jeremy Seifert, "The Church Forests of Ethiopia," video in Op-Doc "What Makes a Church? A Tiny, Leafy Forest," *New York Times*, https://www.nytimes.com/2019/12/03/opinion/church-forests-ethiopia.html.

have for the forest, has preserved them for centuries and possibly longer—Ethiopia is home to some of the earliest Christian
communities.[39] A local Ethiopian Orthodox priest, Aba Gebre
Mariam Alene, expresses beautifully the spirituality associated
with trees: "Every plant contains the power of God, the treasure of God, the blessing of God. So when someone plants a
tree, every time it moves the tree prays for that person to live
longer." [40]

Dr. Wassie is using other church practices to help preserve
the forests. The communities have traditionally built a low wall
around the immediate grounds of the church, to signal sacred
space as adherents approach the church building. Now they
are encouraged to build another, outer wall, surrounding the
forest, to prevent livestock from roaming into the forest and
damaging it. Dr. Wassie sees the church forests as pearls that
might one day be strung together to reestablish forested area
across Ethiopia.[41]

Beyond its biological value, the habitat program shapes a creation consciousness among participants, helping them to appreciate the value of native landscapes. Most Saint Kateri Habitats
include a posted sign identifying the space as such, which raises
awareness among neighbors and passersby. The center's web-
based "story map" of the habitats locates each and provides pic-
tures and a short description. Kateri participant Janet Broderick
of Reston, Virginia, describes her backyard habitat:

> Many animals find shelter and food here: deer, fox,
> squirrels, chipmunks, mice, birds. We are starting to
> recognize the native birds that come to our bird feeder
> and bird bath. . . . We are switching out some of the

39. Goodin, Wassie, and Lowman, "Ethiopian Orthodox Tewahedo
Church Forests."
40. Seifert, "Church Forests of Ethiopia."
41. Seifert, "Church Forests of Ethiopia."

nonnative plants each year. An explosion of daffodils graces our yard every spring followed by red, white, and pink azaleas. I start the day by letting the dog out and making my morning offering while gazing into the backyard and up into the trees (usually with a cup of coffee in hand). What an easy way to drop into a grateful state of mind and soul.[42]

Programs like Saint Kateri Habitat help to lift nature and biodiversity out of the realm of the abstract and into the lived experience and daily consciousness of people of faith.

Another center program, the promotion of "Mary Gardens," elevates the importance of indigenous species by leveraging this traditional Catholic devotion. For centuries, particularly in Europe, the faithful would establish gardens in honor of Mary, many featuring flowers with a scriptural or Marian connection. The center's program encourages the establishment of Mary Gardens across the United States but with indigenous species in place of traditional, nonnative plantings in order to boost native populations in species-poor landscapes such as lawns (see below, 5. The Value of Native Species). The Mary Gardens program encourages participants to consult with local nurseries to ensure that plants used are appropriate to their region, and its website offers native equivalents of traditional Marian flowers.

---

5. The Value of Native Species

Native species introduced at the scale of home yards can increase biodiversity. Doug Tallamy, author of *Bringing Nature Home*, illustrates vividly the power of homeowner choice in selecting plants and trees. He notes that in the mid-Atlantic region, oak trees are host to 534 species of caterpillars—"that's

---

42. "Registered Saint Kateri Habitat Tour," location 41, https://www.kateri.org/story-maps.

534 species of bird food," he clarifies—compared with just one caterpillar species in a nonnative ginkgo tree.[43] Meanwhile, biologist Carol A. Heiser describes the importance of robust habitat for species well-being. She writes that 98 percent of songbirds feed insects to their young, but that an abundant insect population requires a diverse plant community that grows in layers, from leafy mulch and groundcover plants to shrubs, small trees, and oaks or pines.[44] Thus abundant habitat that features native species can be a boon to biodiversity, even at the household level.

LEAVENINGS

Land might be the most visible yet most overlooked asset held by many religious groups. Programs like GoodLands and the Saint Kateri Conservation Center, and the inspirations found in the conservation efforts offered by other faiths, suggest that the potential of faith groups to remediate meaningful swaths of the natural world is significant. Even where lands owned by faith groups are small, they can be part of a necklace of properties across a region that increases the biodiversity and biological resilience of a region. And such programs showcase the importance of folding common-good considerations into our approach to land. This could expand faith interest in community land trusts and other mechanisms of the solidarity economy that remind us that the Earth is a gift for all.

Just as important, programs of land conservation and ecosystem protection help to raise conservation consciousness among people of faith and offer another powerful dimension

---

43. Douglas W. Tallamy, *Bringing Nature Home: How You Can Sustain Wildlife with Native Plants, Updated and Expanded* (Portland, OR: Timber Press, 2009), 107ff.

44. Carol A. Heiser, "Let's Grow Native," *Virginia Wildlife Magazine*, March/April 2019.

in their relationship with God. Working to switch out non-native plants, establish trails, and increase biodiversity can help people to access the secret that St. Francis understood, that we are all part of one grand creation, kin to one another in a spiritually infused natural world. Conservation is good for nature, to be sure, but it is also a boon to our psychological and spiritual well-being. Imagine land appreciation programs and scientific management of property becoming a standard part of faith communities. Their healing impact on a wounded natural world would be huge.

RESOURCES

GoodLands—organization that seeks to map lands held by Catholic institutions as a means for promoting their proper management, www.good-lands.org.

Interfaith Rainforest Initiative—organization that advocates for an end to tropical deforestation and for protection of forests' indigenous guardians, https://www.interfaithrainforest.org.

Living Planet Index—a measure of the world's biological diversity, as part of the Living Planet Report put out by the World Wildlife Federation, https://livingplanetindex.org/home/index.

Saint Kateri Conservation Center—organization that encourages conservation of wildlife habitat, often at the household scale, as a means for protecting and learning to appreciate the living world, www.kateri.org.

Tallamy, Doug, *Bringing Nature Home* (Portland, OR: Timber Press, 2007).

Part III

The Consumption Connection

Consumption is the *and* in "the cry of the Earth and the cry of the poor," the conjunction that links the environmental and social dimensions of the sustainability challenge. In excess, consumption is called consumerism, and it drives environmental destruction. When insufficient, consumption is known as poverty. Consumption occupies the middle ground in this volume because it reaches back and ahead; it is a bridge with two directions of travel, each leading eventually to a damaging state. The good news is that counterefforts to curb consumption in excess can deliver a twofold benefit, healing people and nature alike. For this reason, chapter 7 gives special emphasis to consumerism.

In *Laudato Si'*, Pope Francis levels a clear critique of consumerism for its environmental impact, lamenting that societies regularly find "new ways of despoiling nature, purely for the sake of new consumer items."[1] The impact of consumerism in the Global North is so great that Francis speaks of an "ecological debt" owed by developed countries in the Global North to devel-

1. Pope Francis, *Laudato Si': On Care for Our Common Home* (Vatican City: Libreria Editrice Vaticana, 2015), no. 192.

oping countries whose forests, mines, and soils are depleted and whose air and water are polluted because of the appetites of the Global North. He quotes Pope Benedict in arguing that technologically advanced societies should be prepared to adopt "more sober lifestyles."[2]

Francis is equally critical regarding the social impact of overconsumption. He cites the bishops of New Zealand as asserting that excessive consumption by the wealthy robs the poor of the basics for survival; the bishops even consider whether "thou shall not kill" should be directed to the globally wealthy because of our overconsumption.[3] And Francis critiques societal priorities by contrasting heavy investment in consumer technologies with minimal commitments to resolving urgent societal problems.[4]

Francis demonstrates the long reach of consumerism when he notes that the impact of consumer-driven economies extends well beyond the environment and the poor to the realm of culture and spirituality. He notes that excessive consumption has a leveling effect on cultures,[5] skews our understanding of freedom,[6] leads to spiritual emptiness,[7] and causes us to lose sight of the common good.[8] Indeed, consumerism is a wide-ranging, insidious, and powerful foe.

But Pope Francis is hopeful in the face of such power that "no system can completely suppress our openness to what is good, true and beautiful, or our God-given ability to respond to his grace at work deep in our hearts."[9] He sees spirituality

2. Pope Francis, *Laudato Si'*, no. 193.
3. New Zealand Catholic Bishops Conference, "Statement on Environmental Issues" (September 1, 2006).
4. Pope Francis, *Laudato Si'*, no. 192.
5. Pope Francis, *Laudato Si'*, no. 144.
6. Pope Francis, *Laudato Si'*, no. 203.
7. Pope Francis, *Laudato Si'*, no. 204.
8. Pope Francis, *Laudato Si'*, no. 204.
9. Pope Francis, *Laudato Si'*, no. 205.

and relationship, with the Earth and with each other, as the best tools for dismantling consumerism's power over us. "If we feel intimately united with all that exists, then sobriety and care will well up spontaneously."[10] Recapturing the joy of relationship and the freedom that comes from shedding unneeded possessions rids us of enslavement and opens us to genuine happiness.

10. Pope Francis, *Laudato Si'*, no. 11.

7

Consumerism

In 2012, the PBS program *American Experience* aired "The Amish," a series about the distinctive communities of farmers and craftspeople in Pennsylvania and other states who are renowned for their simple lifestyles and deep faith. Community members stand out: their horse-and-buggy transport, simple clothing, hand tools, and manual labor mark them as people who live fundamentally differently from the majority of U.S. society. So unusual is the Amish lifestyle that sightseeing buses ferry summer tourists to Amish country for a glimpse of their daily life.

One episode of the PBS series reported a revealing exchange between a group of tourists and an Amish man. The tourists asked the man how the Amish are different from them. The Amish man posed three questions in reply:

"How many of you have television?" All the tourists' hands went up.

"How many of you, if you have a family, think you'd be better off without television?" Nearly all the tourists raised their hands.

"How many of you are going to go home and get rid of it?" No hands were raised.

The Amish man's conclusion surely stung: "That's the difference between you and the Amish. . . . If it's bad for the family, we will not have it."[1]

His story lands with authority—not as a masterful critique of television owning; that was not the man's purpose—but because of his quick and effortless proof that the Amish hold a steadfast commitment to their professed values and that the tourists, by their own naked admission, do not. Indeed, the stereotype of the Amish as a people who live without this or that misses the point. The deeper lesson is that the Amish *choose* their lifestyle, guided by a set of internal community values. What a contrast to industrial society, where consumption is shaped heavily by external stimuli, especially advertising.

The point is clearer if we look at Amish use of technology. The Amish are often said to shun technology, but the truth is that they are "techno-selective," using gadgets within boundaries they set for themselves.[2] A new technology—electricity or cars decades ago, or cell phones today—is introduced to the community by early adopters, and its use may spread over time. Members observe the technology's impact with a critical eye. Is the new technology increasing contact with the outside world? Is it weakening community bonds? Is it promoting a sense of pride among users? Eventually, to assess the technology in light of a code of conduct known as the *Ordnung*, members summarize these concerns with a key question: *"Does this technology bring us together or draw us apart?"*

The question is stark, but the answers are often shaded in gray. For example, electricity is fine, but no more than is generated by a twelve-volt battery: access to the full electric grid might encourage purchase of consumer goods that promote pride and

---

1. "Frontline," March 1, 2012, 2:30am–3:30am EST, https://archive.org/details/WETA_20120301_073000_Frontline/start/1080/end/1140.
2. Howard Rheingold, "Look Who's Talking," *Wired* 7, no. 1 (1999), www.wired.com.

envy. Similarly, telephones are allowed, but only in common areas accessible to multiple families, to avoid the disruptions to family life that in-home phones might bring. In short, the Amish accept some technology but only when circumscribed by Amish values. Put differently, the *Ordnung* trumps the market: where the market uses supply and demand to *drive* consumption, promoting acquisitiveness in the process, the *Ordnung* wields biblical values to *limit* consumption, in the process tempering the purchase and use of goods.

The point for people of faith today is not to imitate the Amish lifestyle but to mimic Amish integrity in living their professed values. Faith traditions have a wide range of scriptural and teaching sources that warn of the corrupting power of money and material goods (see below, 1. Spiritual Power, Material Challenge). Yet who could tour retail outlets, listen to a day's worth of advertising, or rummage through Americans' trash cans then conclude that we in wealthy countries hew closely to those teachings? Can we learn to be as true to our ideals as the Amish are to theirs?

---

1. Spiritual Power, Material Challenge

The challenge of consumerism poses a huge paradox: on the one hand, faith institutions have a long history of teaching, dating to founding Scriptures, about the proper role of materialism, money, and wealth. Arguably on no issue from the sustainability agenda do faith groups have as much experience as on teaching about materialism. On the other hand, the secular environmental community, for all its success in raising consciousness and changing policy on a host of environmental issues, has little to show in persuading masses of people to live more simply. On paper, it seems that people of faith can assist. Bill McKibben once wrote, "Among the institutions of our society, only the communities of faith can still posit some reason for human existence other than the constant accumulation of stuff."[3]

---

3. Bill McKibben, "Returning God to the Center," in *The Consuming*

Yet, despite a long heritage of teaching on materialism and consumerism, faith communities themselves have a good deal of remedial work to do on the issue. The truth is that we people of faith are, arguably, as captive to the allure of materialism as any other group in America. As we look to our own teachings for intellectual guidance, the Amish stand out as models of a community worthy of study, a community that dares to live its values.

The Upside of Consumption

The human family passed a historic threshold in 2018 when researchers at the Brookings Institution in Washington, DC, determined that, for the first time ever, half of the world's people could be classified as middle class or wealthier.[4] The landmark moment meant that the daily grind and fight for survival that long defined life for most humans, extending back many millennia, no longer applies to the majority of us. Half or more of the human family has some discretionary income—access to conveniences like motorbikes, refrigerators, and washing machines; and enough financial cushion to survive an economic shock.[5] The researchers forecast continued growth of the middle class into the future (see Table A) to the point that the middle classes of China and India will be approaching the level of wealth found in the United States.[6]

Passion: Christianity and the Consumer Culture, ed. Rodney Clapp (Downers Grove, IL: InterVarsity Press, 1998), 44.

4. Homi Kharas and Kristofer Hamel, "A Global Tipping Point: Half the World Is Middle Class or Wealthier," Brookings Institution, September 27, 2018, www.brookings.edu.

5. Kharas and Hamel, "A Global Tipping Point."

6. Kharas and Hamel, "A Global Tipping Point."

A. Growth of the Global Middle Class[7]

Numbers of Middle Class	Threshold Arrival	Years to Reach Threshold
1 billion	1985	150
2 billion	2006	21
3 billion	2015	9
4 billion	2022	7
5 billion	2028	6

Consistent with these findings, the World Bank reports that the number of poor in the world declined substantially by 2015 from a quarter century earlier. In 1990, one-third of the global population was extremely poor, living on less than $1.90 a day, but by 2015 the share of extremely poor had fallen to just 10 percent, largely due to the rapid increase in prosperity of China and other Asian nations—a huge improvement in human welfare in the blink of an eye. (Notably, however, the impact of COVID-19 is expected to reverse some of these gains. The World Bank reports that the COVID-19 recession will drive up poverty rates for the first time in more than two decades, erasing nearly all the advances in poverty reduction made between 2015 and 2020 and driving some 40 to 60 million people below the threshold for extreme poverty once again.)[8]

The growth of the global middle class is clearly good news for those who have climbed out of poverty. The newfound ability to cover basic needs and to generate enough surplus to make life more comfortable and convenient can only be a godsend for those long mired in poverty. The gains of the once-poor in health, education, life expectancy, and other quality-of-life

7. Homi Kharas, "The Unprecedented Expansion of the Global Middle Class: An Update," Brookings Institution, 2017, 11, www.brookings.edu.

8. World Bank, "Poverty," https://www.worldbank.org.

dimensions deserve vigorous protection. The advance of the global middle class, however, is not an unmitigated success. The advance of the middle class, if driven by a strong consumerist thrust, will pose major challenges for the planet and its people.

THE PLANETARY TOLL

An expanding global middle class (along with increasing consumption levels in wealthy nations) means greater pressure on the environment. The full suite of sustainability issues that make headlines—from climate change to water scarcity to deforestation and species loss—are driven largely by modern patterns of consumption. As long as economies are structured to be materials-intensive (not a requirement, but the reality in all industrial economies today), the environmental impact of greater consumption over much of the planet will be huge. In economies powered by fossil fuels and with little material reuse and recycling, extending middle-class status to the remaining poor of the world would essentially double the environmental impact—twice as many carbon emissions and twice as much soil erosion, deforestation, and air pollution, for example. This is occurring at a time when most societies acknowledge the urgent need to *reduce* human demands on the environment. Clearly, curbing the appetite to overconsume needs to be part of environmental stewardship moving forward.

Waste is emblematic of the unsustainability of industrial economies; in the natural world the waste created as creatures consume is absorbed easily by the environment. But for industrial economies, waste generation is a large and growing problem on land, sea, and air. High-income countries—home to 16 percent of the world's people—account for about a third of the world's waste.[9] The United States stands out among high-income countries where the average citizen generates 87 percent more waste than Europeans.[10] And we generate nearly *five times* as much as the average sub-Saharan African.[11]

Visuals may convey the size of the waste problem better than numbers. Imagine, for example, these three phenomena as symbols of a waste problem out of control:

- *Marine "garbage patches"*—vast collections of trash, mostly plastic, that follow ocean currents and gather in great oceanic gyres. The Great Pacific Garbage Patch makes the news, but in truth five great gyres of marine debris exist, two in the Pacific, two in the Atlantic, and one in the Indian Ocean. The patches are not merely surface phenomena but extend deep below into the sea, where they are known to harm marine life.[12]

- *Atmospheric "brown clouds"*—massive areas of air pollution that hang over various regions, such as the Asian brown cloud over Pakistan, India, Southeast Asia, and China. Brown clouds are harmful to human health, of course, but they also exacerbate climate change and can lead to diminished sunlight and reduction in crop yields of 20 to 40 percent.[13]

- *Coastal "dead zones"*—coastal waters off six continents where rivers carrying fertilizer runoff from farms empty

9. Silpa Kaza et al., *What a Waste 2.0: A Global Snapshot of Solid Waste Management to 2050* (Washington, DC: World Bank, 2018), 3.

10. Kaza et al., *What a Waste 2.0.*

11. Kaza et al., *What a Waste 2.0.*

12. "Garbage Patches," Marine Debris Program, National Oceanic and Atmospheric Administration, https://marinedebris.noaa.gov.

13. Sumit Sharma, Liliana Nunez, and Veerabhadran Ramanathan, "Atmospheric Brown Clouds," Environmental Science, in *Oxford Research Encyclopedias*, https://oxfordre.com.

into the ocean, feeding organisms that consume oxygen and leave little for fish and other denizens.[14] The dead zone at the mouth of the Mississippi River is about *the size of New Jersey.* It is one of five hundred dead zones worldwide.

These outsize examples of our material waste, emissions waste, and farm waste indicate the massive resource inefficiencies of industrial economies today. Yet they are only the tip of the waste iceberg. The world's economies ask the land, seas, and air to absorb far more than even these three egregious examples suggest. And the flow is set to increase: a 2018 World Bank report estimates that waste generation will increase by 70 percent by 2050, growing at more than twice the rate of population growth.[15]

The reality is that industrial economies today are *designed* to allow waste. In contrast to the economies of nature and of traditional indigenous peoples, industrial economies are built on an acceptance that rivers of solid, liquid, and gaseous waste will flow to landfills, the atmosphere, and waterways—even after pollution-control technologies reduce the flows. This is because allowing cars to spew exhaust and sewage to spill into rivers is cheaper (in the short run) than not allowing it. This is a problem of the economic system—pollution seems cheaper because market prices do not factor in the cost of damage done to the environment or people. It is not a problem that can be solved simply by changing individual habits. Creating clean economies in which fewer materials are used and nearly all materials circulate will require new rules for our economy—in addition to a new ethos around consumption.

14. National Oceanic and Atmospheric Administration, "Large Dead Zone Measured in Gulf of Mexico," August 1, 2019, https://www.noaa.gov; area of New Jersey from U.S. Census Bureau, "State Area Measurements and Internal Point Coordinates," https://www.census.gov.

15. Kaza et al., *What a Waste 2.0.*

CONSUMPTION VS. CONSUMERISM

People need to consume to survive. Indeed, consumption must *increase* among the world's poorest people if they are to build lives of dignity. But when consumption becomes an end in itself, it can be labeled consumerism. More precisely, says Amitai Etzioni, a sociologist at George Washington University, when we use purchases not merely to meet our basic survival and security needs but in an ongoing effort to satisfy needs for affection, self-esteem, and self-actualization—there we find consumerism. An example is buying a car to boost self-esteem. Etzioni calls consumerism "a social disease,"[16] an addictive and corrosive force that twists the values of the well-to-do and skews resources away from those in need. Pope John Paul II expressed the critique in spiritual terms in *Centesimus Annus*: "It is not wrong to want to live better," he writes. "What is wrong is a style of life which is presumed to be better when it is directed towards 'having' rather than 'being,' and which wants to have more, not in order to be more but in order to spend life in enjoyment as an end in itself."[17]

Yet consumerism is all around us. Etzioni has written that consumerism has become "the organizing principle of American life." Canadian ecologist David Suzuki observes that people are now defined primarily as customers or consumers, and secondarily as parents, teachers, or voters.[18] American historian Gary Cross has written that consumerism dominated the twentieth century; it proved capable of reorganizing the lives of billions of

---

16. Amitai Etzioni, "The Crisis of American Consumerism," *Huffington Post*, December 6, 2017.

17. John Paul II, *Centesimus Annus*, no. 36.

18. David Suzuki, "Consumer Society No Longer Serves Our Needs," David Suzuki Foundation website, https://davidsuzuki.org, January 11, 2018.

people, without coercion.[19] And in a strong challenge to people of faith, David Loy writes that because shopping and consuming provide meaning to so many people worldwide, consumerism could rightly be called the first truly global religion.[20]

THE SPIRITUAL TOLL

Living to consume introduces a surprisingly long list of distortions to our lives, each with its own spiritual toll. First, consumerism has the power to *displace God* in our hierarchy of loyalties. Thomas Merton wrote that consumerism is nothing less than idolatry; we create false gods as we prioritize accumulation over spiritual growth. In consumer-driven economies, Merton observed, this idolatry is pervasive, and "it is almost completely unrecognized precisely because it is so overwhelming and so total. It takes in everything."[21] Thus, despite Jesus's clear warning that we "cannot serve two masters" (Matt 6:24), consumerism stands as a powerful competitor to God for the allegiance of many.

In allowing ourselves to be defined primarily as consumers, we *downgrade our identity* as children of God. Instead, we are defined according to our prowess in acquiring and using goods.[22] The true security that comes in knowing God's unconditional love for us is obscured and replaced by anxiety as we compare our warehouse of goods to that of our peers. In relaxing our grip

19. Gary Cross, *An All-Consuming Century: Why Commercialism Won in Modern America* (New York: Columbia University Press, 2000), 7.

20. David Loy, "The Religion of the Market," *Journal of the American Academy of Religion* 65, no. 2 (1997): 275–90.

21. Thomas Merton, *A Vow of Conversation: Journals 1964–1965*, ed. Naomi Burton Stone (New York: Farrar, Straus, Giroux, 1988), 174.

22. Cardinal Blase Cupich, "Our Contribution to the Synod of October 2015," *Chicago Catholic*, April 5, 2015.

on the stuff of our lives and learning to rest in the knowledge of God's love, we reclaim our birthright as children of God.

Love of consumption also *distracts from the here and now.* In *Laudato Si'*, Pope Francis wrote that "a constant flood of new consumer goods can baffle the heart and prevent us from cherishing each thing and each moment," denying us innumerable points of access to God.[23] Such distraction also leads us to overlook nature, an instinctive gateway to God. Indeed, St. Francis's simple lifestyle and his love of nature were connected. Pope Francis observes that the saint's austerity was more radical than a mere expression of asceticism; it was *"a refusal to turn reality into an object simply to be used and controlled."*[24] Consumerism teaches us to objectify the world around us, thereby keeping us from grounding ourselves in nature's wonders.

Consumerism distorts our *understanding of freedom* by equating it with extensive market choice.[25] Television ads teach us that we can "have it all," and that we "deserve" a new car or sofa. The average supermarket offers more than 33,000 items for sale.[26] Stores are open at all hours and online shopping puts a planet's worth of goods at our fingertips. The guiding philosophy in consumerist societies might well be "I shop, therefore I am." Yet Franciscan Richard Rohr warns that the siren of expansive choice is spiritually deadening. "'I choose, therefore I am' creates self-absorption and narcissism," he writes, before shifting the spiritual center of gravity: "'I am chosen, and therefore I am,' creates saints and mystics."[27]

---

23. Pope Francis, *Laudato Si'*, no. 222.
24. Pope Francis, *Laudato Si'*, no. 222.
25. Food Marketing Institute, "Supermarket Facts," https://www.fmi.org.
26. Food Marketing Institute, "Supermarket Facts."
27. Richard Rohr, "We Should Ask Why So Few Transformations Happen in Church," *National Catholic Reporter*, March 28, 2003.

Economies driven by consumerism *turn our values inside out.*
The historian and social critic Lewis Mumford noted in 1956
that industrial economies had turned the seven deadly sins—
pride, envy, anger, sloth, avarice, gluttony, and lust—into vir-
tues, because they are useful for selling goods and promoting
economic growth. (For example: identify which of the seven
sins is driving the next commercial you see or hear.)[28] Shortcomings that once drew scrupulous self-examination are now
commonplace and even integral to the economic air we breathe,
with virtually no commentary or protest. Indeed, mainstream
American acceptance of these values as engines of economic
activity stands in sharp contrast to the Amish, whose commitment to spiritual values is steadfast.

As a path of accumulation, consumerism *veers us away from
the path to God.* A former bishop of London, Richard Chartres,
used the story of St. Francis to make this point. Francis was
born into a wealthy merchant family, a family accustomed to
accumulation. But his desire for God led him to abandon his life
of high consumption. Instead he renounced everything—literally stripping off his clothes in front of his bishop—and chose a
life of simplicity. Reflecting on Francis's choice, Chartres wrote:
"We move toward God by subtraction, rather than accumulation." Yet consumerist cultures argue otherwise. Imagine a
television commercial promoting a life of subtraction, urging
viewers *not* to acquire, *not* to compete, to share our goods, to
quiet down and simply listen.

Finally, and paradoxically, to the extent that consumerism
is driven by greed, it *deprives us of plenty and community.* St.
Ambrose reasoned that greed creates scarcity, and exaltation of
private property reduces the stock of common property, a foun-

28. Lewis Mumford, *The Transformations of Man* (New York: Harper &
Brothers, 1956), 104.

dation for community life. The birds of the air have "unfailing nourishment," in part because their world is not divided and owned. God showers them with plenty even though they do not sow. Thus, Ambrose concludes that "avarice must be the cause of our need."[29] Reintroduced today, this line of thinking might raise the question whether consumerist societies overemphasize private consumption—weekends at the mall—and undervalue public consumption—investment in parks, community concerts, and public transport, for example.

TEACHINGS AS A COUNTERWEIGHT TO CONSUMERISM

In *Laudato Si'*, Pope Francis quoted Pope Benedict's diagnosis of the ills that have befallen our planet. "The external deserts in the world are growing, because the internal deserts have become so vast," Benedict declared.[30] Humanity's spiritual emptiness has led us to seek fulfillment in the stimulating but ultimately unfulfilling material world. Pope Francis offers a prescription for this illness. He proposes a lifestyle that allows for "deep enjoyment free of the obsession with consumption" and recommends that we:

> Take up an ancient lesson, found in different religious traditions and also in the Bible. It is the conviction that "less is more.". . . Christian spirituality proposes a growth marked by moderation and the capacity to be happy with little. It is a return to that simplicity which

29. Charles Avila, *Ownership: Early Christian Teaching* (Eugene, OR: Wipf & Stock, 1983), 72–73.

30. "Homily of His Holiness Benedict XVI: Mass, Imposition of the Pallium and Conferral of the Fisherman's Ring for the Beginning of the Petrine Ministry of the Bishop of Rome," April 24, 2005, http://www.vatican.va.

allows us to stop and appreciate the small things, to be grateful for the opportunities which life affords us, to be spiritually detached from what we possess, and not to succumb to sadness for what we lack. This implies avoiding the dynamic of dominion and the mere accumulation of pleasures.[31]

Indeed, so deeply human is such wisdom that it is found widely among the world's faith traditions (see below, 2. Selected Religious Perspectives on Consumption). As widespread and popular as the pull of consumerism is, it is met with a low-key but powerful counter tug: the spiritual call to a life deeper and richer than the one promised in thirty-second TV ads.

---

2. Selected Religious Perspectives on Consumption

Bahá'í Faith—"In all matters moderation is desirable. If a thing is carried to excess, it will prove a source of evil." (Baha'u'llah, *Tablets of Baha'u'llah*)

Buddhism—"Whoever in this world overcomes his selfish cravings, his sorrows fall away from him, like drops of water from a lotus flower." (*Dhammapada*, 336)

Christianity—"No one can be the slave of two masters. . . . You cannot be the slave both of God and money." (Matthew 6:24)

Confucianism—"Excess and deficiency are equally at fault." (Confucius, XI.15)

Daoism—"He who knows he has enough is rich." (*Dao De Jing*)

Hinduism—"That person who lives completely free from desires, without longing . . . attains peace." (*Bhagavad-Gita*, II.71)

Islam—"Eat and drink, but waste not by excess: He loves not the excessive." (Qur'an, 7.31)

Judaism—"Give me neither poverty nor riches." (Proverbs 30:28)

---

31. Pope Francis, *Laudato Si'*, no. 222.

A QUESTION OF SOLIDARITY

Who in the developed world has not questioned the justice in having so much while hundreds of millions of people are chronically hungry? Indeed, inequality has nagged consciences for centuries, often drawing the interest of church leaders. Early leaders' views on inequality are astonishingly demanding for today's reader (but no more demanding than passages from the Gospels). In a blunt statement that could have been written as recently as 2018 as migrants entering the United States were being caged, St. Ambrose, an archbishop of Milan in the fourth century, exclaimed: "There is your brother, naked, crying, and you stand there, confused over the choice of an attractive floor covering." [32]

Ambrose was not alone in this framing. Listen to St. Basil the Great, also a fourth-century bishop, from a sermon to the wealthy of his community about ownership:

> That bread which you keep, belongs to the hungry; that coat which you preserve in your wardrobe, to the naked; those shoes which are rotting in your possession, to the shoeless; that gold which you have hidden in the ground, to the needy. [33]

Ambrose and Basil give us the rawest criticisms of ownership. Stripped away are considerations of different eras, different economic systems, and all the caveats that muddy the ethical waters around how we consume. Ambrose and Basil clarify the morality of property by reducing the question to two people: the suffering one and me—just as Jesus did in the story of Lazarus and

32. "The Christian Quotation of the Day," Friday, December 7, 2018, http://www.cqod.com; more formal translation at Charles Avila, *Ownership: Early Christian Teaching* (Eugene, OR: Wipf & Stock, 1983), 65.
33. Avila, *Ownership*, 50.

the rich man. For the materially saturated, the tale of Lazarus and the accusations of Ambrose and Basil make for uncomfortable reading, indeed.

But these and other fourth-century faith leaders root their teachings in something deeper than a sense of mercy. It is also a question of community and of justice: the world is the common inheritance of all, and we have no right to hoard. As Ambrose states: "It is not from your own goods that you give to the beggar; it is a portion of his own that you are restoring to him. The Earth belongs to all. So you are paying back a debt and think you are making a gift."[34] Today, for those whose economies are often grounded in the right to private property, this critique lands harshly. But Ambrose and Basil were hardly alone. Saint John Chrysostom, another fourth-century Christian bishop, makes the same point, equally pointedly: "What you give is not yours but your Master's, common to you and your fellow-servants. For which you ought especially to be humbled, in the calamities of those who are your kindred."[35] So much for feel-good charitable giving!

Of course, economies today *are* radically different from those of the fourth century and caveats *are* in order. The industrial era has unleashed a torrent of goods and services that, to a growing share of the world, offer better health, lives free of hunger, and education that opens doors to realizing one's fullest potential. We can be grateful for these advances. But vast inequalities still exist, and the critiques of Ambrose, Basil, and John Chrysostom may be even more relevant today. After all, they were evaluating the elites of their day, the people who possessed surplus wealth; but surplus wealth in the twenty-first century is commonplace in many societies. Members of the middle class are not off the

34. Avila, *Ownership*, 66.
35. Avila, *Ownership*, 98.

hook just because their wealth is Lilliputian compared to that of Jeff Bezos, Mark Zuckerberg, and Bill Gates.

Indeed, church teaching still insists that wealth is not entirely a private affair. It uses the term "universal destination of goods" to suggest that creation is a common inheritance. And, while it acknowledges a right to private property, that right is far more circumscribed than is commonly understood; in fact, private property is "subordinated to the right to common use."[36] Owners of production must make their property fruitful and use it to benefit others.[37] "Goods of production—material or immaterial—such as land, factories, practical or artistic skills, oblige their possessors to employ them in ways that will benefit the greatest number," says the *Catechism of the Catholic Church*. Meanwhile, consumers are charged to use their goods "with moderation, reserving the better part for guests, for the sick and the poor."[38] We are not chastised for enjoying the comforts of modern life but instead are urged to view our consumption in the larger context of social need and environmental health.

THE SUSTAINABILITY RESPONSE TO CONSUMERISM

Sustainable development offers solutions to excessive consumption that are promising but ultimately inadequate. One way to reduce the ever-increasing materials load of the global economy, especially as more people grow more prosperous, is to create "circular economies"—essentially zero- or minimal-waste economies that mimic the economy of nature. The concept extends well beyond recycling to embrace innovations for delivering

---

36. *Compendium of the Social Doctrine of the Church*, 177, www.vatican. va.

37. *Catechism of the Catholic Church*, §2404, www.vatican.va.

38. *Catechism of the Catholic Church*, §2405.

what people need, with the lowest material footprint possible. In a circular economy, goods are designed to last or to be disassembled and remanufactured, extending their useful lives. Or they are replaced by services, as when a shared car from Zipcar replaces the need for one's own car. Products in a circular economy are made of "biological nutrients" that can be recycled or returned safely to the biosphere (e.g., compostable tableware), or they are "technical nutrients" such as metals that can also be recycled. And a circular economy is assumed to run on renewable energy. The circular-economy concept offers a tantalizing vision of economies that capture many of the advances of industrial society while living in balance with the Earth.

Nevertheless, sustainability solutions are likely incomplete in addressing overconsumption. Many intriguing circular-economy concepts have yet to be tried and proven. And traps may hide within otherwise exciting solutions. Consider the rebound effect—the idea that savings from more efficient consumption in one area may be spent on greater consumption elsewhere. If I buy a more gas-efficient car, feel more flush because of my lower fuel bill, then boldly fly off to Nassau for a beach vacation that I would not otherwise have taken, the carbon burden on the environment may actually increase.

Indeed, it is a mistake to think that greater efficiency necessarily means a cleaner economy. This misconception results from confusing efficiency with conservation. Efficiency refers to using less of something relative to something else, such as less gasoline per kilometer traveled. Conservation refers to using less absolutely. Andy Rudin of the Interfaith Coalition on Energy is clear about the need for more conservation, advising congregations to turn things off and forgo their use where possible. Rudin appreciates the Amish because of their emphasis on conservation rather than efficiency, which gives them a far lighter environmental footprint than their neighbors who use energy-efficient appliances and machines.

Missing from sustainability solutions to overconsumption is any effort to address the spiritual deprivation that overconsumption represents. Here faith communities, assisted by psychological insights, can be helpful. Psychological research suggests that relationships are central to a person's happiness and can be more important than income. One study found that doubling the number of friends has the same impact on a person's reported well-being as a 50-percent increase in income.[39] Faith communities might explore what more they can do to bring people together in meaningful relationship, whether within congregations or across a city.

Faith communities might also consider what they can do to put flesh on their many teachings regarding consumption. A simple model for personal consumption comes from the indigenous Tlingit people of Alaska. The Tlingit use the bark of cedar trees as an economic resource, even for clothing. They see the bark not in instrumental terms but as part of the sacred world that we all inhabit. Thus, before peeling away bark from a tree, they make a prayer of thanks to the tree's spirit and promise only to use as much of it as they really need. What a model! Imagine if, every time we pulled out a piece of paper, flipped on a light switch, and started a car, we gave thanks to God for the gift we are about to use and promised only to use as much as we really need. How much deeper would our appreciation of the natural world be, and how much less would we engage in mindless consumption.

39. John F. Helliwell and Haifang Huang, "Comparing the Happiness Effects of Real and On-Line Friends," *PLoS One*, September 3, 2013, https://www.ncbi.nlm.nih.gov.

Leavenings

Faith communities are more strongly positioned than almost any other institution to tame the consumerist impulse that drives so many economies today. Faith precepts are available to teach simple living, stewardship of resources, and the importance of the common good and community building. These lessons can combat the individualist notion that "we live to consume." But these lessons have impact only if we take them as seriously as the Amish take to heart their faith values.

Asking people to consume less is neither easy nor popular. But faith communities have largely not played their most powerful card: unmasking consumerism as ultimately unsatisfying and revealing that communities of strong relationships are a worthy competitor to consumerism. Faith communities might critically evaluate their own patterns of consumption and ask if their material profile could be trimmed to bear witness more faithfully. Then they can design enticing models of community activity that build relationships, deemphasize unnecessary consumption, and expand people's true freedom. Achieving this, and multiplying it across faith communities nationally, would transform our economy more profoundly and positively than almost any other single initiative.

Resources

Avila, Charles. *Ownership: Early Christian Teaching*. Eugene, OR: Wipf & Stock, 1983.

Cross, Gary. *An All-Consuming Century: Why Commercialism Won in Modern America*. New York: Columbia University Press, 2000.

Etzioni, Amitai. "The Crisis of American Consumerism." *Huffington Post*. December 6, 2017.

Loy, David. "The Religion of the Market." *Journal of the American Academy of Religion* 65, no. 2 (1997): 275–90.

Murphy, Monsignor Charles. "The Good Life from a Catholic Perspective: The Challenge of Consumption." Washington, DC: USCCB, 2014.

Part IV

The Cry of the Poor

An objective reading of *Laudato Si'* leaves little doubt that Pope Francis's economic vision diverges sharply from the reality of many modern economies. He is unimpressed with GDP and other isolated measures of wealth; he critiques a wasteful "super development" and calls for a new progress that is "healthier, more human, more social, more integral."[1] He rejects "a magical conception of the market" and the profit motive as insufficient for building economies of dignity.[2] He even questions the notion of economic growth, an untouchable concept in most governments, noting that "the time has come to accept decreased growth in some parts of the world, in order to provide resources for other places to experience healthy growth."[3]

Francis believes it is time "to develop a new economy, more attentive to ethical principles."[4] He offers glimpses of an alternative economy: "cooperatives of small producers" who opt for cleaner means of produc-

1. Pope Francis, *Laudato Si'*, no. 112.
2. Pope Francis, *Laudato Si'*, no. 190.
3. Pope Francis, *Laudato Si'*, no. 193.
4. Pope Francis, *Laudato Si'*, no. 189.

tion and for "a non-consumerist" way of life;[5] land ownership for rural people, in addition to access to technical education, credit, insurance, and markets;[6] and intelligent ways to expand reuse and refurbishment of products, and recycling of materials.[7] In short, Francis writes, societies need "a sustainable and equitable development within the context of a broader concept of quality of life."[8] This new vision would be "a worthy expression of our most noble human qualities."[9]

People of faith can help to build such an economy. The four chapters in this section, on innovations in social enterprise, investment, fair trade, and local finance, cover a few examples of economic innovation that advance the cause of sustainability. They could easily be supplemented with chapters on worker co-ops, which have had strong Catholic support over the past century, and other elements of the "solidarity economy," such as cooperative housing, community land trusts, and public banks. But the four chapters give a sense of the role that people of faith already play in helping to hear the cry of the poor. These idealistic, but real, economic options are built on the same optimism that led Francis to exclaim that "an authentic humanity, calling for a new synthesis," is penetrating modern cultures "like a mist seeping gently beneath a closed door."[10] Economic structures that are pro-poor can open the door and welcome this authentic human spirit.

5. Pope Francis, *Laudato Si'*, no. 112.
6. Pope Francis, *Laudato Si'*, no. 94.
7. Pope Francis, *Laudato Si'*, no. 192.
8. Pope Francis, *Laudato Si'*, no. 192.
9. Pope Francis, *Laudato Si'*, no. 192.
10. Pope Francis, *Laudato Si'*, no. 112.

8

Social Enterprise

Reverend Becca Stevens, a survivor of sexual abuse, has developed a passion for healing. She works to heal abuse victims in Nashville, where she lives, but also women across the country, and even impoverished women overseas. She sees a wounded Mother Earth and desires to mend her, too. Healing is her vocation: over three decades, Stevens, an Episcopal priest, has created a unique and effective abuse-recovery ministry. But it is a ministry with a look and feel unlike any other.[1]

Stevens is the founder and president of Thistle Farms, which sells home and body products, from candles and lotions to placemats, clothing, and jewelry. It is a social enterprise, an organization that uses a market engine to drive a social mission. That mission is "to help women survivors recover and heal from prostitution, trafficking, and addiction" by providing "a safe place to live, a meaningful job, and a lifelong sisterhood of support." Some seventy-five survivors of abuse work at the Thistle Farms factory, offices, and café.[2] Many live in five residential homes around Nashville, in a two-year program that covers rent and

---

1. John Yang and Leah Nagy, "How this Nashville Women's Recovery Home Blends Business with Bonding," *NewsHour,* November 1, 2019, www.pbs.org.

2. Becca Stevens, email to author, June 8, 2020.

other costs so the women can focus on their own healing. More than 80 percent of Thistle Farms' management team is women.

The organization's products communicate care; many carry the logo *Love Heals Every Body*. "I wanted to make something healing for the body," Stevens explains. "Women's bodies, the collective body, the Earth body. We went back to essentials, like oils, which are mentioned in 425 scriptural passages." The products are ethically sourced, justice inspired, and sustainably produced from simple recipes. "They are healing for the customer, for the women who made them, for the community, and for the Earth," she concludes.

The more you learn about Thistle Farms, the longer its social tentacles seem to extend. Stevens has built a network of healing around the organization, for example, by partnering with thirty organizations in twenty countries to produce fair-trade products for sale through Thistle Farms—all made by survivors of abuse. Survivors of sex trafficking in Cambodia create bags and flowerpots, women with disabilities in India make textiles, and survivors of the Rwandan genocide produce tea and baskets.[3] Partnering organizations pay their workers at least 25 percent above the minimum wage for their country and invest in local social programs focusing on health care, vocational training, child care, food security, agriculture development, and other initiatives.[4]

Meanwhile, in the United States, Thistle Farms has assisted in the establishment of fifty organizations across the United States that use the Thistle Farms model of recovery. Half of these now have residential homes for women, while the others

---

3. "Global Partners," Thistle Farms, https://thistlefarms.org/blogs/global-partners.

4. "Global," Global Factsheet, https://cdn.shopify.com/s/files/1/1795/6929/files/TF_Global_Website_PDF.pdf?2629878210905127342.

are in earlier stages of development. Legally independent, they are affiliates of Thistle Farms in that they belong to an aligned network that shares core principles, ideas, resources, language for grant applications, and more, a sharing ethic that facilitates the spread of healing.[5] "Remember, justice is a noncompetitive sport," Stevens says in summarizing her sharing philosophy.

Environmental care is part of the Thistle Farms ethos as well. The home and body products are not tested on animals, the cafe offerings are sourced from organic farms, and the enterprise is exploring options for packaging made from recycled materials. For Stevens, integrity across the enterprise is important. A fair-traded tea that helps women farmers but is not produced organically, she observes, would "break the chain of healing" and would not be acceptable.

In sum, the organization's pathways of healing stretch from its Nashville center to suppliers overseas to affiliated organizations in the United States, with customers being the glue that holds it all together. It is a broad network of solidarity with women and with nature. Indeed, more than a *social enterprise*, Thistle Farms might be described as the center of a proto *social economy*, an economy of well-being.

Imagine the Thistle Farms model replicated across the country. The demand certainly exists; in Nashville alone, a hundred women are on the waiting list to enter the Thistle Farms residential program. And many social concerns in addition to abused women could potentially benefit from the many flavors of social enterprise that exist today. Could communities of worship help create economies of well-being in locales across the nation through support of innovations like social enterprise?

5. Becca Stevens, conversation with author, April 6, 2020.

A Hybrid Business

Social Enterprise Alliance defines social enterprises as "organizations that address a basic unmet need or solve a social or
environmental problem through a market-driven approach."
Social enterprises can be for-profit or nonprofit firms; some even
provide social services normally associated with governments.
For-profit social enterprises often focus on making money, then
using profits to fund a social cause. Nonprofit social enterprises
make social benefit the DNA of their operations. An example is
the Girl Scouts, whose cookie sales fund a large share of organizational expenses to support the development of young girls.

Certainly, Thistle Farms is a business, providing goods and
services in a market setting. But it also mimics government in its
provision of a safety net—the subsidized housing it offers women
seeking to reenter the workforce. And it has the feel of a nonprofit
in the job training and counseling it provides. Indeed, while Thistle Farms is legally structured as a nonprofit, its functions straddle
the three sectors. And in its straddling, the enterprise expresses
values that many would recognize as Gospel inspired.

Profit-seeking, Nonprofit, or Compassionate Business?

The blurred lines between social purpose and profit making
prompt questions about the social-enterprise model. Can a
profit-dependent business seriously pursue social goals? If profit
making stalls, what gets abandoned—the social service or profit
seeking? Alternatively, should a nonprofit with a clear social
mission be charging for services? Answers to these questions will
vary according to the type of social enterprise, as suggested in
the examples below.

Despite confusion over the nature of social enterprise, proponents make a strong case for the concept. Nonprofit funding is often tenuous in a world of government budget cuts and short-term philanthropic commitments; earned revenue can provide greater security for good works than grants. In addition, a social enterprise offers the dignity of a meaningful job to its employees; many of the women at the Thistle Farms factory and café stress the boost to self-esteem that having a job gave to them. And where social enterprises charge clients for services, clients are arguably invested in the outcome and take the service seriously.

The size of the sector is difficult to track because definitions of social enterprise differ widely across countries. In 2018, the trade organization Social Enterprise UK (SEUK) reported that social enterprises accounted for 3 percent of GDP and 5 percent of employment in the United Kingdom.[6] And the sector appears to be robust. SEUK reports that nearly three-quarters of social enterprises in the United Kingdom made a profit or broke even in 2019.[7] And more than half introduced a new market or service in 2019, compared with just over a third of conventional small and medium enterprises.[8] Social enterprises certainly face difficulties, including difficulty accessing capital, the perception that social enterprises offer inferior goods and services, and the belief that they are more fragile and more likely to go out of business. Yet, proponents note that policies to level the playing field can help address these challenges. Furthermore, some of the concerns are not warranted: British research shows that the top one hundred social enterprises in the United Kingdom that

6. "Hidden Revolution: Social Enterprise in 2018," (London: Social Enterprise UK, 2018), www.socialenterprise.org.uk.

7. Claire Mansfield and Dan Gregory, "Capitalism in Crisis? State of Social Enterprise Survey 2019," Social Enterprise UK, 2019, www.social enterprise.org.uk.

8. Claire Mansfield and Dan Gregory, "Capitalism in Crisis? State of Social Enterprise Survey 2019," www.social enterprise.org.uk.

were in business since 1984 were no more likely to fail than the one hundred largest conventional businesses.[9]

Are the Thistle Farms of the world merely niche solutions—impressive innovations, to be sure, but perhaps too difficult to replicate and spread? The jury is still out, but interest in creating businesses that add social, not just financial, value is clearly on the rise. Social Enterprise UK reported in 2019 that two out of five social enterprises were under five years of age, triple the share for small and medium enterprises overall.[10] And the management consulting firm McKinsey says that publications focused on social enterprise increased in number from twenty-seven to well over five hundred in the decade leading to 2016. If interest is any indicator, the unrealized potential for injecting social good into business activity would appear to be strong.

Certainly, many social issues do not have a market solution. It is hard—no, outrageous—to imagine a soup kitchen charging homeless people for a meal. Government programs and pure charities will always be needed for issues that are too large or that fit markets too poorly. But properly defined and supported, social enterprise may be an untapped option for advancing the common good in innovative, dignified, and sustainable ways.

Religious Interest

Social enterprise in its simplest forms has long existed in many houses of worship. Think of the parish thrift shop, typically a small outfit that leverages donated goods and volunteer labor to create a low-overhead store whose profits become revenues for the parish. That's a simple social enterprise. At the other extreme is the Mondragón complex of worker cooperatives in

9. E3M, "Who Lives the Longest? Busting the Social Venture Survival Myth," http://socialbusinessint.com.
10. Mansfield and Gregory, "Capitalism in Crisis?"

Spain, founded by a Catholic priest in 1956 who was interested in worker justice; it is now the tenth largest company in Spain and has operations on five continents.[11] The examples suggest that faith groups pursue social enterprises of wildly different kinds, for a broad variety of purposes.

In 2017, Catholic Charities USA (CCUSA), the largest Catholic social service agency in the United States, made social enterprise and workforce development one of seven strategic priorities for its five-year plan.[12] The move was motivated by CCUSA's concern over growing inequality and insecurity of employment; the organization saw social enterprise as a promising tool for fighting poverty.[13] The CCUSA network is large, with 167 local offices that oversee 2,600 social service facilities serving more than 12 million people, so its decision was significant.[14] By 2018, some 50 social enterprises were run by Catholic Charities agencies, generating a total of $36.5 million in revenues.[15]

Some Catholic Charities social enterprises, such as The Refuge Café in Phoenix, approach the business-and-benefit sophistication of Thistle Farms. Founded in 2013, The Refuge serves a variety of breakfast and lunch items, along with specialty coffees, smoothies, and other drinks at its downtown and airport locations. It also offers online ordering for home delivery. Patio seating complements indoor space, and a conference room for community or business meetings is also available.

But the café's full value proposition extends well beyond food and socializing. Its coffee is made from ethically sourced beans

11. https://www.mondragon-corporation.com.

12. Steve Bogus, communication with author, August 13, 2019.

13. Matt Zieger, "An Economy That Works for All," *Charities USA*, Spring 2018, 7.

14. "One in Dignity, One in Love," Annual Report 2018 (Alexandria, VA: Catholic Charities, 2018).

15. "One in Dignity, One in Love."

from farmers associated with the Rainforest Alliance. The beans are roasted by veterans who once struggled to find employment; many live in housing provided by Catholic Charities. Some café staff are youth aging out of foster care, for whom a job is a welcome blessing. Arts and crafts made by refugees from around the world are sold in a small shop on site. And profits from the café fund Catholic Charities programs that support foster children, veterans, refugees, and survivors of domestic violence. Consequently, The Refuge is an ongoing lifeline for dozens of people each year as it fills a market niche for thousands of customers. Like Thistle Farms, The Refuge demonstrates that a retail business can be an engine of assistance for vulnerable populations, even as it operates successfully in a market environment.

Creating small businesses like Thistle Farms and The Refuge is not easy, and their retail-as-social-service-provider model cannot solve all social problems. Stephen Capobres, vice-president of business development at Catholic Charities Community Services of Arizona, notes that creating a business that competes directly with for-profits requires the same discipline and attention to quality and reliability required of any business. "People may visit you once because you are supporting a social service," Capobres remarks, "but if they are not getting a good product or service, they won't come back."

Indeed, values beyond revenue generation may be more important in some social enterprises. For Mike Melara, CEO of Catholic Charities of the Diocese of Syracuse, New York, a chief objective is to provide meaningful work, which he calls "the best antidote to poverty." His agency's Project Joseph, a property maintenance business, provides jobs or job training to hard-to-employ populations; it charges for services in the market, but revenues don't necessarily cover all its costs. "We don't see these projects as a way to bring resources into Catholic Charities," he explains. He notes, too, that if profit is the goal of a project, as it must be at Thistle Farms and The Refuge Café, "it leads to different kinds of decision making. You think differently than if your goal is to keep people employed." Melara is not partial to one form of social enterprise over another. "You just have to be clear about what your goal is," he explains.

Project Joseph undertakes tasks from light repair and maintenance to painting, cleaning, lawn service, and snow removal. It also does odd jobs—small and difficult jobs that no other businesses want to do, "like moving three tons of stone from one side of an apartment complex to another," explains Melara. The Project began as a charitable program of Catholic Charities, but in 2019, it was converted into a limited liability corporation, with a board separate from that of Catholic Charities.[16]

Its dozen or so employees are often people whose pasts make them hard to place in a job. More than half are clients of Catholic Charities—beneficiaries of their programs, such as their homeless shelter. Some will move on to jobs in the private sector, but others are likely to be with Project Joseph their entire working lives. All receive the same pay, which is greater than the minimum wage.

Project Joseph competes in the open market for various kinds of work. In the spring of 2020, it had eighty-three separate snow removal contracts and eight landscaping contracts. Booked business at that time totaled $250,000, with bids out on another dozen projects worth $1 million. Project Joseph is still a startup business whose expenses exceed revenues, with foundation grants or Catholic Charities helping to plug shortfalls. Whether Project Joseph will be self-sufficient in the long run is an open question, even though overhead has been kept to 10 percent.

16. Mike Melara, communication with author, March 9, 2020.

Regardless, Melara is clear that the social side of the Project Joseph ledger is irrefutably in the black. Employees have pride in their work and in their uniform. "They show up every day. They like being part of the team. They don't want to let each other down," Melara says. Put simply, they find dignity in being a Project Joseph employee, a return on investment that cannot be expressed as a percentage or dollar value. For Melara, the social return is the real gold in Project Joseph.

B. Examples of Social Enterprises at Catholic Charities[17]

Program	The Service	Charging	Leveraging	Benefitting (social/ market)
Catholic Charities Fort Worth Dental Clinic	Dental Care	Recipients	Paid dental professionals	Low- and moderate- income families
Transportation with Purpose Fort Worth	Transportation to work, school, medical, quality of life appointments. (The program provides over 80,000 trips annually.)	People who need rides	Volunteer drivers	Low- and moderate- income people
Translation and Interpretation Network Fort Worth	Document translation, American Sign Language interpretation, and language consulting services	Recipients	Language skills of immigrants	Immigrant populations with language proficiencies

---

17. Fort Worth, https://www.catholiccharitiesfortworth.org; Kansas City, https://catholiccharitiesks.org/new-roots-for-refugees.

The Culinary Arts for Self-Sufficiency (CASS) Onondaga County	Five-week training in culinary skills, and catering services	Recipients	Catholic Charities (CC) services	Hard-to-employ persons/ entities that need catered food and frozen entrees
Project Joseph Onondaga County	Trains recent refugees and men struggling with homelessness in basic property maintenance.	Recipients	CC services	Hard-core unemployed/ entities that need work done
LOOM Chicago	Provides a platform for refugee women to create and sell their handmade products, as well as training in financial literacy and other services	Purchasers of goods	CC services	Refugees who need work/ market purchasers
Refuge Café Phoenix Catholic Charities Community Services	Serves ethically sourced coffee. Beans are roasted, packaged by veterans at a coffee roaster inside a temporary living facility. The café also sells hand crafts and art made by refugees	Purchaser of goods	CC services	Refugees, veterans/ customers

New Roots for Refugees Catholic Charities of Northeast Kansas	Helps refugee families to start small organic farm businesses that sell through farmers' markets and wholesale to local restaurants	Purchasers of produce	CC provision of land	Refugees/ Customers

LOCAL HUBS OF RELIGIOUS ENTREPRENEURIALISM

Catholic Charities has the advantage of a national network of agencies who share their experiences of social enterprise. But other faith groups have successfully set up enterprise groups as well:

Central Detroit Christian Community Development Corporation (CDC)—With a focus on rebuilding a city devastated by neglect, CDC offers educational and job-training programs to empower and lift the morale of poor citizens. It also has seeded ten social enterprises, including Peaches and Greens, a produce shop; Detroit re-Made, which recrafts and repurposes abandoned materials and products; Fit and Fold, a laundromat with a small gym, as well as firms that provide landscaping, security, property management, and other services.[18]

Belay Enterprises—A group of business people and pastors in the Denver area work to create businesses to employ and train people afflicted by addiction, homelessness, and prison records. These include Baby Bud's, a thrift store for baby products; Freedom Cleaning Services, a commercial building-services company launched in 2003; and Good Neighbor Garage, which rehabilitates donated vehicles for use by low-income families.

18. https://www.centraldetroitchristian.org.

It also started a Venture Partner's Program to assist other faith venture start-ups.[19]

Homeboy Industries—This initiative to combat gang activity in Los Angeles was founded by the Jesuit Greg Boyle and includes companies like HomeGirl Café, Homeboy Electronics Recycling, Homeboy Silkscreen and Embroidery, and several others. The Homeboy model has attracted attention to the point that it created the Global Homeboy Network to "create therapeutic communities that offer job skills training, cost-free programs and services, and social enterprise employment." More than four hundred organizations are part of the network.[20]

Interest in faith-based social enterprises is great enough that a firm called Mission Incubators has formed to help churches think about their missions in innovative ways. "It's the church's job to find every means possible to reflect Christ's love in the world and to turn harebrained ideas into sustainable forms of mission and impact," says their website. "Not only do we think impact entrepreneurship is possible through churches and those who lead them—we think this is where ministry is headed, especially where young people are involved."[21]

GROWING THE SECTOR

Faith-based networks of social good can promote the spread of social enterprise. A good example is collaboration between the Miller Center for Social Entrepreneurship at Jesuit-run Santa Clara University, which works to "accelerate" social entrepreneurship in the United States and abroad, and Innovation

19. https://belay.org.

20. https://homeboyindustries.org.

21. "Why Are We Doing This?" Ministry Incubators, https://ministry incubators.com.

Works, a Jesuit-inspired nonprofit in Baltimore that works to create sustainable neighborhood economies through training and mentoring for social enterprise.

Both organizations are ambitious. The Miller Center's vision is to "accelerate entrepreneurship to end global poverty and protect the planet," while Innovation Works focuses its effort locally, aiming to transform Baltimore by launching and nurturing 250 social enterprises over ten years that will employ 5,000 people, mostly African-American and Latino, in low-income neighborhoods in the city, attracting $100 million in investments in the process (see below, 3. From Prison to Employment). It does this, in part, by involving Jesuit institutions from around the city, including the Ignatian Volunteer Corps and the Maryland Province of the Jesuits, and Catholic Charities of Baltimore.

---

3. From Prison to Employment

One of the enterprises being nurtured by Innovation Works is a nonprofit organization called The Chill Station, which was established to create jobs for formerly incarcerated persons returning to communities in Baltimore. It has created a program called Lifting Labels: Changing Lives with Each Stitch to produce clergy and choir robes and judicial gowns. The idea is straightforward: former inmates have a high unemployment rate, but some are skilled sewers because of their experience in prison sewing shops. Lifting Labels taps these skills to create meaningful work for such hard-to-employ persons. Its champion, Rev. Chester France, is a former insurance executive, minister, and prison chaplain, whose business experience and understanding of the needs and promise of former inmates equip him to shepherd the Lifting Labels vision to reality.

Reverend France participates in a Miller Center/Innovation Works program that has helped him to develop a business plan, including an investment pitch to funders for $200,000; other capital will come from foundation grants and sales revenues.

He expects to rent a portion of a shared workspace, install sewing machines, hire five persons to produce a small batch of robes as a proof of concept, then scale up production. Reverend France projects that the business will be self-supporting by the end of the third year of operations.

Reverend France sees real potential for the program. Many churches have prison ministries and will understand the value of helping former inmates. Some might contribute to The Chill Station as part of their social outreach ministry. Others might order robes from Lifting Labels. The organization could be popular among congregations who appreciate knowing that those who were formerly incarcerated will be home and able to build a career with confidence and stability. Support for Lifting Labels' reentry initiative could multiply across denominations.

The Miller Center/Innovation Works collaboration offers a hint of the potential for social enterprise. Far from providing charity alone (which has its own value and remains critically necessary in other circumstances), the collaboration suggests that faith organizations can create a different kind of economy, featuring programs, services, and enterprises that exist for purposes beyond profit generation. Faith groups have the capacity to inject grant funding when needed but also the entrepreneurial skills to create ongoing enterprises. The combination offers a nimbleness to create businesses of compassionate purpose within a structure of market discipline.

LEAVENINGS

Social enterprise raises fundamental questions about the purpose of private companies, and whether they can do more to advance social and environmental values. It also prompts thinking about the work of charities and whether they might function more entrepreneurially to generate more secure funding. Answers to these questions are complicated and depend on context. But exploration of them increases the possibility of creating a fairer and more resilient economy.

Congregations and faith organizations need not create businesses, although as noted, many already have a simple social enterprise on site in the form of a thrift shop. But faith communities might wrap their ethical minds around the nature of businesses and organizations around them. Innovations from the solidarity-economy world are many. On the production end, producer co-ops, democratic employee stock ownership plans, and worker co-ops are worth exploring. For consumers, there are consumer co-ops, ethical purchasing clubs, and housing co-ops available. Expanding ideas regarding the nature of enterprise could raise consciousness around the purpose and functioning of the economy as a whole, and stimulate thought regarding how economies might be made fairer.

RESOURCES

Catholic Charities USA (CCUSA)—runs social enterprise programs across the United States, https://www.catholiccharities usa.org.

Miller Center—promotes social enterprise as an antipoverty tool in the United States and abroad, https://www.millerso cent.org.

Social Enterprise Alliance—is an association promoting social enterprise in the United States, https://socialenterprise.us.

9

Investment

In 2001, the 178-strong Franciscan Sisters of Mary (FSM), a religious community in the Midwestern United States, faced an uncertain future. With no lasting recruits in twenty years, an average age in the seventies, and a cavernous motherhouse that was more burden than benefit, the order questioned its very viability.[1] What was God calling the community to, after nearly 130 years of heroic service across the Midwest? Meeting in a congregation-wide assembly, the sisters prayed and explored options for their future, then took a momentous decision: the community would end its recruitment of new members and follow the Spirit regarding next steps. "With that decision," reads the account on the order's webpage, "we as a congregation accepted the reality that our community would come to an end sooner rather than later."[2]

To be clear, the sisters did not pack up and close their doors. Not at all. Steeped in the faith that had sustained them for generations, the women asserted that while the *community* of sisters would soon be gone, the *order* would remain and transition to "a new way of being." To shape their new structure and set its

1. Rose M. Dowling, FSM, Irma Kennebeck, FSM, and Sandy Schwartz, FSM, "Transformed into a New Way of Being," internal document, (Bridgeton, MO: Franciscan Sisters of Mary, 2017).

2. https://www.fsmonline.org.

path, the sisters set out to read the signs of the times and to pray intensively. Moved by the urgency of the climate and sustainability crisis, they added a clarifying new emphasis to their mission statement—"compassionate care of Creation in collaboration with others."[3] After selling the motherhouse, accounting for the retirement and health needs of the remaining sisters, and helping congregational employees to transition to new work, the order held investment assets that could advance its mission long after the sisters were gone.

But as then structured, the order's investments did not match the ethical ambition of their creation-care mission. The sisters would need to upgrade from their respectable but limited investment strategy of targeting *good firms* to funding *impactful work*.[4] "In 2009 our investing doors blew wide open when we discovered 'impact investing,'" reports the FSM website. The reference is to investments that aim for clear social and environmental impact, in addition to financial returns. Guided by their new commitment to compassionate care of creation, the FSM community divested their holdings of fossil-fuel stocks[5] and restructured their investments to include impact investments that promoted climate stability and advanced the UN's Sustainable Development goals.

In spring 2019, only fifty-five FSM sisters remained—more than half of whom were over eighty years old—and the sisters held their final chapter meeting and elected their last leadership team.[6] The meeting was bittersweet, to be sure, but the sisters

3. The key to the order's new way of being was its investment portfolio.

4. "Why Faith-based Organizations are Shifting to Impact Investing," Knowledge @ Wharton, https://knowledge.wharton.upenn.edu., November 1, 2018.

5. Dowling, Kennebeck, and Schwartz, "Transformed into a New Way of Being," 20–22.

6. "Final FSM Chapter," *FSM Magazine*, Summer 2019.

emerged joyful and confident that their "new way of being," built around a set of assets and activities designed to build a more just and environmentally healthy world, was set in place.

It is hard to say what is most admirable in the sisters' story: their courage in taking a very painful step, their trust that God would see them through a moment of existential crisis, or their imagination in setting a new direction for the order. Indeed, FSM courage, trust, and creativity are a powerful collective example to people of faith today. We, too, are called to a new way of being—to hear the cry of the Earth and the cry of the poor—that will require us to take painful steps to remake economies and life-styles. We are challenged to trust that God will support us in these steps. And we, too, may find that our assets, including any investments, can be better configured to create societies based on justice, dignity, and living in harmony with the Earth.

Undo Harm

As the FSM Sisters understood, an important early step in ethical use of wealth is to use "negative screens" to shed investments that run counter to one's values.[7] This action has a long history among religious groups. Quakers in the nineteenth century spearheaded the Free Produce Movement, a boycott of cotton cloth, sugar, and other products produced with slave labor.[8] In the early twentieth century, Quakers and other groups

---

7. Negative screening means excluding companies that do not comply with specific, preset social or environmental criteria. Examples are mutual funds that exclude companies involved in the production of alcohol, tobacco, or gambling products, also referred to as "sin stocks." Other negative screens frequently applied are on weapons manufacturers, nuclear power producers, or companies that use child labor.

8. Willy Blackmore, "The Boycott's Abolitionist Roots," *The Nation*, August 14, 2019, www.thenation.com.

rejected investments in alcohol, tobacco, and other so-called "sin stocks."[9] By the 1980s, religious divestment efforts were targeting companies doing business in South Africa in support of a worldwide movement against apartheid,[10] as well as corporations that build nuclear weapons.[11] Today, a large share of divestment work focuses on fossil-fuel companies because of the damage done to the climate by the combustion of coal, oil, and natural gas. Many involved in divestment also use another strategy, stakeholder engagement, to influence corporate behavior, although this may not be as useful for fossil-fuel companies as for other types of businesses.

Indeed, fossil-fuel divestment is on a tear. Portfolios divesting of fossil-fuel holdings were valued at $50 billion in 2014[12] but reached an estimated $14 *trillion*[13] just six years later—a 280-fold growth. (Dollar values refer to the total value of portfolios that have divested, not the value of the divested stocks, which is typically proprietary information.) More than a thousand institutions, from faith groups and philanthropies to educational institutions and pension funds, are part of the divestment movement.[14] Of particular note is the sovereign development fund of the Republic of Ireland, whose 2018 divestment announcement

9. "Responsible Investing: Aligning Personal Values with Investing Dollars," Highland Financial Advisors, 2018, 2, www.highlandplanning.com.

10. Chelsie Hunt, Olaf Weber, and Truzaar Dordi, "A Comparative Analysis of the Anti-Apartheid and Fossil Fuel Divestment Campaigns," *Journal of Sustainable Finance & Investment* 7, no. 1 (2017): 64–81.

11. "Divestment of Nuclear Weapons," International Campaign to Abolish Nuclear Weapons, April 2020, https://www.icanw.org.

12. 2014 from Arabella Advisors, "Measuring the Growth of the Global Fossil Fuel Divestment and Clean Energy Investment Movement," October 2016 at https://www.arabellaadvisors.com.

13. Fossil Free, "1000+ Divestment Commitments," https://gofossilfree.org.

14. Fossil Free, "1000+ Divestment Commitments."

was the first by a national government.[15] And of great symbolic importance was the 2014 divestment decision by the Rockefeller Brothers Fund, whose wealth came from Standard Oil, a predecessor to today's ExxonMobil.

Religious groups are at the leading edge of the fossil-fuel divestment movement, accounting for nearly a third of divested institutions.[16] GoFossilFree lists some 397 religious institutions that have divested of fossil fuels.[17] Global Catholic Climate Movement, which tallies Catholic divestment activity, lists 191 Catholic institutions that have divested as of June 2020,[18] including 25 that divested in a May 2020 group rollout to mark the fifth anniversary of *Laudato Si'*.[19] The Catholic institutions include religious orders, dioceses and archdioceses, and Catholic lay institutions and banks.

C. GROWTH IN DIVESTMENT, BY SECTOR, 2014 AND 2020[20]

Sector	Share of Divestment (percent)	
	2014	2020
Faith Institutions	2	32
Philanthropic Institutions	8	15
Educational Institutions	38	15
Government Institutions	48	13
Pension Institutions	0	13
Others	4	11

15. Yossi Cadan, Ahmed Mokgopo, and Clara Vondrich, "11 Trillion and Counting," https://financingthefuture.platform350.org.

16. Fossil Free, "1000+ Divestment Commitments."

17. https://gofossilfree.org.

18. https://catholicclimatemovement.global/divest-and-reinvest/leaders/.

19. https://catholicclimatemovement.global/divest-and-reinvest/leaders/.

20. 2014 data from Arabella Advisors, "Measuring the Global Fossil Fuel Divestment Movement," https://www.arabellaadvisors.com; 2020 data from Fossil Free, "1000+ Divestment Commitments."

THE CASE FOR DIVESTMENT

The case for shedding fossil-fuel investments is a strong one—morally, financially, and legally. The moral argument is made succinctly by the advocacy organization 350.org: *If it is wrong to wreck the climate, it is wrong to profit from that wreckage.*[21] This disarming logic is rooted in questions of justice. Those most likely to suffer from climate change live in the tropics—typically in poor countries that did the least to cause the climate problem, benefited little from fossil-fuel use, and are least equipped to defend against climate catastrophes, a triple injustice.[22] Perhaps more outrageous in terms of justice, because of its willfulness, is the determination of fossil-fuel companies to search for *more* carbon-based resources despite the climate crisis and serious underfunding of the clean-energy sector.[23] Thus, the moral case for divestment is strong and arguably evocative of the scandals that sent the prophets of ancient Israel into the streets screaming for justice.

Divestment from fossil fuels may also make financial sense; a case that is supported by simple math. Limits to temperature increase set by the global community translate to limits on the burning of fossil fuels, which creates a "carbon budget"—the amount of carbon the human family can release into the atmosphere without busting through globally agreed temperature caps. In 2011, the energy finance think tank Carbon Tracker presented a simple but powerful analysis: the carbon content in

21. https://gofossilfree.org/about-fossil-free.

22. Human Development Report 2019, 179, http://hdr.undp.org.

23. Alex Lenferna, "Divest-Invest: A Moral Case for Fossil Fuel Divestment," Oxford Scholarship Online, n.d. doi:10.1093/OSO/97801 98813248.003.0008.

the coal, oil, and gas reserves of leading energy firms was several times greater than the carbon budget allows.[24]

In other words, energy firms held, as assets on their books, large quantities of fossil fuels that for moral and legal reasons should never be burned and that therefore are at risk of being abandoned. Carbon Tracker estimates that under a scenario limiting warming to 1.6 degrees Celsius, 83 percent of capital expenditures on new oil projects between 2019 and 2030 are unneeded and at risk of being written off.[25] Because such "stranded assets" would no longer represent potential earnings, their loss would lower the value of company stock. And the risk to investors only grows as corporations search for more oil and gas and add more unburnable assets to their books.

Finally, divestment makes sense to avoid the financial fallout of companies' legal liability for climate damage. Documents have surfaced showing that companies like ExxonMobil knew about the climatic impact of their businesses in the early 1980s, putting them potentially at legal risk for untold damages.[26] Other companies, like the German energy company RWE, are being sued because of material damage to a Peruvian farmer whose farm is increasingly vulnerable to flooding because of warming-driven glacial melt.[27] Still others, like the environmental group Urgenda in the Netherlands, have sued the Dutch government—successfully—for its failure to honor

24. "Unburnable Carbon: Are the World's Financial Markets Carrying a Carbon Bubble?" Carbon Tracker, July 13, 2011, carbontracker.org.

25. Andrew Grant and Mike Coffin, "Breaking the Habit: Why None of the Large Oil Companies Are Paris-Aligned, and What They Need to Do to Get There," Carbon Tracker, September 2019, 4, carbontracker.org.

26. Steven Felt, "Trillion Dollar Transformation: Fiduciary Duty, Divestment, and Fossil Fuels in an Era of Climate Risk," Center for International Environmental Law, December 2016, 22–25, www.ciel.org.

27. Felt, "Trillion Dollar Transformation," 22–25.

climate commitments, charging that this failure was a violation of human rights.[28]

Despite the moral, financial, and legal arguments for divestment, and in the face of rocketing commitments to divest, fossil-fuel companies are largely doubling down on their climate-damaging business models. The Transition Pathway Initiative (TPI), a project that assesses company readiness for the transition to a low-carbon economy and is supported by several churches, found in a 2020 report that only two of fifty oil companies are aligned with the Paris Climate Agreement targets,[29] an echo of findings from Carbon Tracker in 2019 that the major oil companies continued to back projects that are not Paris-compliant.[30] And the banking industry is largely not helping. A 2020 report from the Sierra Club and other activist organizations found that, while some banks are restricting fossil-fuel financing, funding continues to surge.[31] Some thirty-five private sector banks have poured *$2.7 trillion* into fossil-fuel finance *since the international community adopted the Paris Agreement* in 2015.[32] Andrew Grant, an author of the Carbon Tracker report, summarized the situation: "Every oil major is betting heavily against a 1.5°C world and investing in projects that are contrary to the Paris goals."[33]

28. Felt, "Trillion Dollar Transformation," 22–25; John Schwartz, "In 'Strongest' Climate Ruling Yet, Dutch Court Orders Leaders to Take Action," *New York Times*, December 20, 2019.

29. Simon Dietz, "TPI State of Transition Report 2020," Transition Pathway Initiative, March 2020, www.transitionpathwayinitiative.org.

30. Grant and Coffin, "Breaking the Habit."

31. "Banking on Climate Change: Fossil Fuel Finance Report 2020," Rainforest Action Network, March 18, 2020, www.ran.org.

32. "Banking on Climate Change."

33. Grant and Coffin, "Breaking the Habit."

Invest in Good

Divestment is only one face of the ethical investing coin. The other is to invest in any number of goods and services designed to build a more just and sustainable world—using divested funds or new funds—in a field known as "impact investing." Impact investing allows investors to direct their wealth toward projects that will deliver clear social or environmental gains. For example, some impact-investment opportunities are built around the United Nations' seventeen Sustainable Development Goals, which set ambitious targets for ending hunger and poverty, ensuring access to water, providing quality education, stabilizing the climate, ensuring gender equality, and providing access to clean energy, among other goals.[34] Microfinance institutions, community development projects, and investments in clean energy and health access are common targets of impact investing.

Broadly speaking, two major sets of actors are involved in the field. On one side are investors, like the FSMs, but also philanthropic foundations, high-net-worth individuals, and financial institutions, from banks and pension funds to institutions specializing in development finance. On the receiving side are social enterprises, small businesses, and infrastructure projects that seek to deliver social as well as financial returns.[35] Supporting players are also involved, such as NGOs, government programs, and networks.[36]

Interest in the sector is growing, although its size is still modest; the Global Impact Investing Network estimated in 2019 that 1,340 firms managed more than $502 billion, less than

34. Global Impact Investing Network: "Achieving the Sustainable Development Goals: The Role of Impact Investing," https://thegiin.org.

35. "15 Companies Making a Difference with Impact Investing," B The Change, June 1, 2016, https://bthechange.com.

36. "15 Companies Making a Difference."

1 percent of assets under management (invested funds) globally, which totaled more than $70 trillion before the COVID-19 pandemic hit.[37] Yet the fundamental driver of the sector, the desire to ensure that one's wealth is making the world a better place, seems to remain an enduring value.

One subset of impact investing that is of special interest to values investors, including faith investors, is concessionary impact investing. Like all portfolio holders, most impact investors seek a competitive, market rate of return on their investments; the social and environmental gains they value are pursued in addition to market financial returns. But some impact investors understand that projects with high social or environmental returns may generate sub-par financial returns and are willing to accept lower, "concessionary" rates of return. These investments may be enough to seed economic activity that would not otherwise happen and which, in turn, can generate a host of other economic transactions that provide jobs and better lives for people on the economic margins. Thus, concessional impact investing is a sacrificial type of investing that yields impactful social or environmental outcomes and may hold particular appeal to values investors.

Energy Poverty

Although impact investing can benefit a wide range of sectors, we focus here on investments in clean energy. It is a natural complement to fossil-fuel divestment, but, more important, it carries strong potential to reduce poverty in developing countries, a particular interest of faith groups.

---

37. Suzy Waite, Annie Massa, and Christopher Cannon, "Asset Managers with $74 Trillion on Brink of Historic Shakeout," Bloomberg, August 8, 2019, www.bloomberg.com.

In all human civilizations, energy availability shapes economies and development.[38] Consider, on the one hand, the broad array of functions in industrial economies made possible by harnessing energy: lighting, cooking, refrigeration, mechanical power, transportation, heating and cooling, and communications, to name a few.[39] On the other hand, where energy is greatly limited—where nations or regions suffer from "energy poverty" or a low level of energy access—poverty is the sure outcome. Thus, access to energy is critical to development efforts, which is why ensuring access to energy for all by 2030 is one of the United Nations' Sustainable Development Goals (SDGs).

But energy poverty is the norm for billions of people worldwide, and the world is not on track to meet the energy access goals set by the SDGs. Roughly 11 percent of the world's people do not have access to electricity today and 35 percent lack access to clean cooking fuels and technologies[40] (see Table D). While access is expanding, projections indicate that 620 million people will (still) lack access to electricity in 2030.[41]

Ending energy poverty will require solutions that look very different from the centrally generated energy systems found in most of the world. Most people who are energy poor live in impoverished rural areas; meeting their needs for electrification will require inexpensive, decentralized options that can be distributed even in remote regions. The International Energy Agency has estimated that nearly two-thirds of new investment

---

38. Lauren C. Culver, "Energy Poverty: What You Measure Matters," Pre-symposium White Paper for: Reducing Energy Poverty with Natural Gas: Changing Political, Business, and Technology Paradigms, May 9 and 10, 2017, Stanford University, CA, ngi.stanford.edu.

39. Culver, "Energy Poverty."

40. REN21, "Overview of Energy Access," in *Renewables 2020: Global Status Report* (Paris: REN21 Secretariat, 2020), www.ren21.net.

41. "Tracking SDG 7: Affordable and Clean Energy," *The Energy Progress Report*, Energy Sector Management Assistance Program, 2020.

D. Populations Living in Energy Poverty[42]

	Number lacking access (million)	Share of global population (percentage)
Electricity	860	11
Clean cooking fuels and technologies	2,650	35

in energy access will need to be in the form of decentralized technologies such as solar lamps, solar home systems, and solar minigrids. Fortunately, these are increasingly affordable to low-income populations with access to credit. Add small-scale finance such as microfinance, and affordable mobile communications technologies that facilitate commerce and banking, and the ingredients for rapid expansion of energy access may be at hand.

But investment in the renewable energy sector is less than half the level needed to meet the temperature goals laid out by the Paris Agreement in 2015, according to the International Renewable Energy Agency.[43] Moreover, most energy investment today continues to overlook microscale needs, a critical issue in sub-Saharan Africa, where decentralized systems such as solar photovoltaics are the most economical solution for about three-quarters of needed connections—and where they can boost quality of life remarkably (see Table E and 1. The Solar Electricity Advantage).[44] Furthermore, according to the International Energy Agency, investment shortfalls could be worsened by the COVID-19 economic slump, adding to the challenge.[45]

42. REN21, "Overview of Energy Access."
43. IRENA, *Global Energy Transformation: A Road Map to 2050 (2019 edition)* (Abu Dhabi: International Renewable Energy Agency, 2019), www.irena.org.
44. https://www.iea.org/access2017.
45. International Energy Agency, "The Impact of the Covid-19 Crisis on Clean Energy Progress," June 11, 2020, www.iea.org.

E. HIERARCHY OF RENEWABLE ENERGY TECHNOLOGIES[46]

Technology	Applications	Significance
Rechargeable solar lamps	Household lighting	Solar-powered lights promote education and create a pollution-free home environment, improving health
Stand-alone solar home system	Cellphone, radio and TV	These technologies connect individuals to the larger community; cellphones create options for enterprise and banking
Microgrids	Refrigerators, fans, irrigation pumps, small machinery, such as lathes and milking machines	Create income-generating opportunities

---

1. The Solar Electricity Advantage

Investments in simple solar technologies can have a huge impact. The Global Off-Grid Lighting Association (GOGLA), an industry group, has documented these benefits. Using data from more than 2,300 new off-grid solar users in Kenya, Mozambique, Rwanda, Tanzania, and Uganda, the association found that nearly 60 percent of new off-grid purchasers undertook more economic activity within three months of installing new systems. More than a third of these customers saw their income increase by $35 per month, which amounts to more than half the average monthly GDP per person for the five countries.[47] And many families replaced kerosene lamps

---

46. http://theconversation.com/empowering-the-powerless-lets-end-energy-poverty-83628.

47. GOGLA, Altai Consulting, and UKAID, "Powering Opportunity:

with solar lamps, resulting in improved health.[48] Such tangible increases in economic performance and quality of life are the building blocks that spur development advances.

A bottom-up investment strategy could help close the investment gap for reducing energy poverty. Values-driven investments such as impact investing can provide capital for difficult-to-fund but otherwise promising projects. Indeed, impact investors provided 49 percent of the $139 million invested in off-grid solar companies in 2017, making these investors a critical component of the energy-access equation in developing countries.[49]

RELIGIOUS INVESTMENT FOR IMPACT

Religious groups would seem to be a natural constituency for impact investing given their interest in values and in building a better world. But faith groups may be warming to the field only slowly; a 2020 survey of religious institutional investors undertaken by the Global Impact Investing Network suggests that only 11 percent of those surveyed used impact investing as an investment strategy.[50] Yet the survey also demonstrated clear commitment to values investing in other ways: 88 percent of faith respondents use divestment and negative screens, and 61 percent use ESG criteria in their investment strategies.[51] The survey's mixed results, say its authors, suggest that a lack of information regarding impact investment creates caution among faith

---

The Economic Impact of Off-Grid Solar (Executive Summary)," Utrecht: GOGLA, July 2018, www.gogla.org.

48. GOGLA, Altai Consulting, and UKAID, "Powering Opportunity."

49. The 49 percent is a GreenFaith calculation based on data in http://www.ren21.net/gsr-2018/chapters/chapter_04/chapter_04/#sub_5.

50. GIIN, "Engaging Faith-Based Investors in Impact Investing," Global Impact Investing Network, January 2020, https://thegiin.org.

51. GIIN, "Engaging Faith-Based Investors."

institutions, which is perhaps understandable given that impact investing is a relatively new subset of the investment sector.

Still, efforts to promote impact investing among people and institutions of faith continue. The Vatican sponsored three international conferences on impact investing between 2014 and 2018.[52] In 2014, the Catholic Impact Investing Collaborative (CIIC), founded by FSM CEO/CFO John O'Shaughnessy, was created to promote impact investing among Catholic institutions; some twenty-five institutions are now members. As noted, some high-profile initiatives are making headlines, including the 2020 commitment by sixteen congregations of Dominican sisters—along with other congregations interested in values investing, such as the FSMs—to create a $46 million Climate Solutions Fund to address climate and development simultaneously.[53] Meanwhile, a first-of-its-kind interfaith conference on faith investing that was held in South Africa in 2019 helped to advance the field.

2. Islamic Values in Investing

At an international conference in South Africa in September 2019 entitled "Financing the Future," the Fiqh Council of North America released an authoritative Islamic legal ruling, a *fatwa*, in favor of investment in clean energy.[54] It states: "We call upon Islamic investment houses and other investment fund administrators and managers to immediately develop fossil-free

52. John O'Shaughnessy, "Why Faith-Based Organizations Are Shifting to Impact Investing," Podcast, Knowledge @ Wharton, https://knowledge.wharton.upenn.edu, November 1, 2018.

53. Brian Roewe, "Dominican Sisters Commit $46 Million to Seed New Climate Solutions Funds," National Catholic Reporter/EarthBeat, June 18, 2020, ncronline.org.

54. Dr. Muzammil Siddiqi et al., "Statement of Fiqh Council of North America on Fossil Fuel Divestment," August 30–September 1, 2019, https://financingthefuture.global.

investment vehicles and portfolios that include investments in renewable and clean energy companies."

A group of three Muslim organizations in the United Kingdom—the Islamic Foundation for Environmental & Ecological Sciences (IFEES/EcoIslam), Mosques & Imams National Advisory Board (MINAB), and the Bahu Trust—issued a statement in support of the North American action.[55] Their statement noted that "Profiting from fossil fuel production, in its current form, is financially unnecessary, morally wrong and goes against the spirit of the Quranic teachings of environmental stewardship."

Investing in "Last-Mile" Communities

But perhaps the greatest impact in advancing energy access is found with investments in small-scale renewable energy for "last-mile" communities typically overlooked in large-scale energy plans. This is difficult for many reasons: investment opportunities in small-scale projects are often riskier because of their low rates of return. Beneficiaries of investment, typically low-income customers, may be stretched to afford energy products and services, raising the risk of missed payments. And identifying viable small-scale projects can be difficult. These obstacles are formidable, making private investment in last-mile communities a major challenge.

But the opportunity is real, too. Development efforts that engage "last-mile" populations in building energy-access solutions offer a broad range of benefits for families, villages, and societies. Indeed, some argue that few initiatives offer as many

55. "Joint Statement by the Islamic Foundation for Environmental & Ecological Sciences (IFEES/EcoIslam), Mosques & Imams National Advisory Board (MINAB) and the Bahu Trust on Divesting from Fossil Fuels and Investing in Renewable Energy," Joint statement of IFEES/EcoIslam, MINAB, and Bahu Trust, The Global Climate Divest-Invest Summit, September 10–11, 2019, Cape Town, South Africa, https://financingthefuture.global.

opportunities to advance the United Nations' Sustainable Development Goals as energy access. Consider, for example, that energy access:

- *creates economic opportunity,* by greatly expanding options for home- or community-level entrepreneurial activity;
- *increases access to water,* by powering electric pumps that allow for a more consistent water supply, with benefits for health and agriculture;
- *increases food security,* by expanding the use of irrigation, increasing farm yields and food supplies;
- *weakens the stranglehold of extractive industries on development,* by delivering clean energy that is decentralized and affordable;
- *broadens local finance,* by engaging local banks and other sources of capital, thereby strengthening the community's financial base;
- *provides financial power to families,* by creating opportunities for affordable finance and credit-building;
- *protects the climate,* by reducing greenhouse gas emissions and pressure on the climate;
- *protects health,* by eliminating household burning of wood and kerosene for cooking;
- *advances gender equity,* by creating economic opportunities for women;
- *promotes human rights,* by establishing a right to energy access and rights to consent and participation in energy development.

Energy access initiatives offer new opportunities in the global north as well. Impact investors gain the satisfaction of knowing that their investment impact is felt in some of the poorest and most difficult-to-reach areas of the world. And philanthropies are challenged to operate in more collaborative ways with other funders, a prerequisite for successful scaling of energy-access initiatives.

Given the opportunity presented by clean-energy access, its likely appeal to values investors, and the SDG goal of providing energy access to all by 2030, a partnership of religious groups, foundations, and development experts created the Shine Campaign in 2017 to develop a model for bringing energy access to remote areas, especially in Africa and India. Shine is the brainchild of GreenFaith, the Wallace Global Fund, the IKEA Foundation, and Sustainable Energy for All. It also is supported by major faith groups including the World Council of Churches.

The Shine Campaign model is distinct from many other development models. First, the campaign is committed to the last-mile concept and to helping those often overlooked in energy development in rural areas. Second, it insists on participatory development, with affected communities involved in project design from the outset. Participation also means deep involvement of women and indigenous people as well as local project partners in technology, small enterprise, and banking. These commitments place Shine at the center of some of the knottiest challenges in rural development—but this placement, the campaign believes, is what makes remote energy-access possible, with all the economic possibilities this implies. As of mid-2020, the campaign was drawing up plans to scale up its model, a prerequisite for the far-reaching impact at the heart of Shine's ambition.

Leavenings

The experience of the FSMs and the Shine Campaign indicate what is possible when faith values lead an approach to investments. Divestment, shareholder advocacy, and impact investing are tools used by the sisters to deal ethically with their wealth. They pressed their advantage where they could, for example, by integrating a portion of their impact investments into a Climate Solutions Fund set up by sixteen Dominican congregations that promoted climate solutions *and* the United Nations' Sustainable Development Goals.[56] In sum, the FSM sisters seem intent on ensuring that FSM investments, which now represent their legacy, are devoted as fiercely to gospel values as the sisters themselves have been over their 150-year history.

Similarly, faith values animate the Shine Campaign and arguably are what make the campaign so bold—and what may account for its success. The campaign's commitment to helping people on the margins—in this case, last-mile communities—is a value familiar to people of faith, and, for Christians, evokes the shepherd who seeks to find the lone lost sheep. In addition, the longstanding interest in poverty alleviation among people of faith makes the many advantages of decentralized, clean-energy access highly appealing. Moreover, impact investing, especially of the concessionary kind, is likely to be of interest *only* to religious and other values investors, and may provide critical, project-facilitating financing.

People of faith, individually and corporately, sit on trillions of invested wealth dollars. Imagine the impact our investments could have in creating cleaner and more just economies if they were leveraged to advance the values we profess each week.

Resources

Catholic Impact Investment Collaborative—serves Catholic institutional investors to steer wealth in service of people and planet, http://www.catholicimpact.org.

56. Roewe, "Dominican Sisters Commit $46 Million."

Carbon Tracker Project—helps investors to understand the risks of holding stock in companies that sell fossil fuels, https://carbontracker.org.

Fossil Free—advocacy group that works to end the use of fossil fuels and to embrace renewable energy, https://gofossilfree.org.

Shine Campaign—a partnership of faith groups, developers of small-scale renewable energy, and philanthropies that catalyzes development by extending renewable energy to people in remote areas, http://www.shineinvest.org.

Transition Pathway Initiative—helps investors to compare their portfolios against the goals of the Paris Agreement to create a low-carbon economy. Supported by the Church of England, https://www.transitionpathwayinitiative.org.

10

Fair Trade

Virtually every dimension of Mary O'Brien's active life is defined by her faith, including her consumption habits. A committed coffee drinker, Mary buys only fair-trade coffee, paying a premium that benefits poor producers. For Mary, coffee choice is an ethical decision, an act of solidarity with struggling farmers and a concrete expression of an option for the poor, a key tenet of Catholic Social Teaching. Her deep commitment has made her a fair-trade evangelist; she visits half a dozen parishes annually to promote the practice among parishioners, inviting them to incorporate fairly traded coffee, tea, chocolate, olive oil, clothing, and artisan crafts into their parish and personal lives.

Mary's promotion of fair trade draws from a deep well of direct experience. She collaborates with staff members of Equal Exchange, a Massachusetts-based fair-trade company, and has toured its coffee-roasting facility in West Bridgewater. She has traveled to El Salvador to visit the farm cooperative, Las Colinas, whose brewed beans fill her morning mug. In 2012, she and other Americans spent three days with the Sánchez family and eighty-eight other cooperative farm families at Las Colinas. Her group was integrated into daily routines of its hosts, sleeping on the floor, using an outhouse, taking bucket showers, eating little meat, and learning to appreciate a hermit's ration of electricity—enough to power two light bulbs. Mary and her compatriots worked in the fields, helping Mr. Sánchez to plant his crops. She notes wryly that with Mr. Sánchez's deft field skills, he could transplant two hundred seedlings in a day, but with the group's help, he managed to plant fifty!

Mary's understanding of the world of coffee deepened as a result of her trip. Las Colinas was previously a foreign-owned plantation; for Mary, stories of the plantation's harsh conditions and abysmally low pay were evocative of slavery. She contrasted those accounts with the reality of the new cooperative, which, while poor, was clearly a step up; it gave farmers like the Sánchez family a voice in democratic decision making, greater security, and a realistic hope of a university education for their children. Mary also distinguished the cooperative from a third model, a nearby fair-trade plantation, where the workers, in Mary's view, were manifestly worse off than the worker-owners at the cooperative, since workers were not involved in running the operation.

Mary O'Brien's commitment to fair trade is rooted in her faith. "Fair trade covers all seven principles of Catholic Social Teaching, starting with solidarity," she notes with enthusiasm, referring to the cooperative model of fair trade. It also emphasizes the dignity of the human person, the rights of workers, subsidiarity, the option for the poor, "and certainly, care for creation," she observes. She worries that fair trade seems "squishy" at times, for example when it embraces coffee from the corporate-run Salvadoran plantations. And she wishes that genuine fair-trade principles would extend to *all* cross-border commerce. "I really think that if we could more and more embrace the idea of solidarity, then everything we buy from overseas would be fair traded," she observes, her idealism in full bloom. It is an exalted wish, but one that faces serious obstacles. It is a vision that will require the full commitment of many faith partners if it is to come to fruition.

What Is Fair Trade?

Fair trade refers to the production and sale of commodities, like Mary O'Brien's coffee, at a fair price for producers and under conditions designed to protect them and the environment. It also typically includes a premium for community development. In fair trade, advocates see a market-based tool to protect poor farmers in developing countries from erratic price swings, while advancing their development prospects in the process.

---

1. Common Characteristics of Fair Trade[1]

Fair World Project lists these as principles of fair trade agreed to by certifiers and membership organizations:

- direct trading relationships that give farmers enduring access to markets
- fair prices that may be higher than market prices
- no child labor or forced labor
- nondiscrimination in the workplace, gender equity, and freedom of association
- democratic and transparent organizations
- safe working conditions and reasonable work hours
- investment in community development through a premium paid by buyers
- environmental sustainability
- traceability and transparency

The potential of fair trade to help poor farmers is real. Some 65 percent of the world's poor working adults toil in agriculture, often producing commodities whose prices barely support family livelihoods.[2] Many produce coffee, the most traded com-

---

1. https://fairworldproject.org/get-informed/movements/fair-trade/principles/.

2. Andrés Castañeda et al., "Who Are the Poor in the Developing World?" Policy Research Working Paper 7844, Poverty and Equity Global Practice Group, World Bank Group, October 2016, openknowledge.worldbank.org.

modity in the world after oil, and a crop notorious for volatile prices, which makes the life of a coffee farmer precarious.[3] Given that many governments are unable to invest as needed in their agriculture sectors, the potential to invest in farmers directly, through fair prices for their produce, is appealing to many consumers. The food, beverages, textiles, crafts, and other goods imported from developing countries are, in principle, delivery platforms for improving the lives of the distant poor.

Whether that vision can be realized remains to be seen. Despite rapid growth over more than two decades, and despite the fact that 1,700 producer organizations are now certified by the world's largest fair-trade certifier, the original vision of fair trade—a movement that stands in solidarity with poor farmers through relationship-based commerce—is increasingly in peril.[4]

A Promising Start

From its origins, people of faith have helped to define genuine fair trade as a pro-poor movement rooted in solidarity and personal exchange. After World War II, a Mennonite woman named Edna Ruth Byler, taken by the beauty of textiles that were handmade by women in Puerto Rico, began to sell batches of their work in the United States, where the goods could capture a just price. Her efforts eventually led to the founding of Ten Thousand Villages, a retailer that opened its first fair-trade shop in 1958 and that claims to be the largest fair-trade retailer in the United States. Byler's humble self-description—"I'm just a woman trying to help other women"—captures the original,

3. Colleen Haight, "The Problem with Fair Trade Coffee," *Stanford Social Innovation Review*, Summer 2011, https://ssir.org.

4. "Fairtrade Producers Overview," Fairtrade International, https://www.fairtrade.net.

person-to-person idealism of fair trade.[5] Ten Thousand Villages and similar organizations, such as SERRV, are characterized by the small scale of their operations; their artisanal, rather than mass-produced products; and their direct relationships with small overseas suppliers.

Given the success of early efforts at fair trade, advocates sought to scale it so that more poor producers might benefit. In 1988, a Dutch Jesuit, Frans Van der Hoff, and his compatriot, economist Nico Roozen, collaborated with farmers in the UCIRI coffee cooperative in southern Mexico to help them enter the mainstream coffee market. The farmers did not want development aid any longer, Van der Hoff explains, "but a fair price for their coffee at scale."[6] The idea was to move their coffee out of niche "Third World shops," such as Ten Thousand Villages, and into mainstream supermarkets. Fair-trade values in mainstream markets promised the best of both worlds: just prices at mass scale.

The initial entrance ticket to mainstream markets was certification, a label assuring buyers that a product is produced according to ethical standards. Frans Van der Hoff organized the first certification in 1988 with the *Max Havelaar* label on coffee sold in Dutch supermarkets.[7] Consumers in marketing surveys seemed to like the idea of ethically produced coffee but were slow to warm to an alternative brand, and sales hovered at around 2 percent of the coffee market in the Netherlands.[8]

---

5. https://www.tenthousandvillages.com.

6. Nico Roozen, "Organizing Hope: The Founding Fathers of Fair Trade Meet Again," October 29, 2019, LinkedIn.com; Paul T. M. Ingenbleek and Machiel J. Reindeers, "The Development of a Market for Sustainable Coffee in the Netherlands: Rethinking the Contribution of Fair Trade," *Journal of Business Ethics* 113 (2012): 461–74.

7. Roozen, "Organizing Hope Again."

8. Roozen, "Organizing Hope."

Consumer interest was real, however, and once name brands became involved, fair-traded coffee took off. Today, certified products amount to more than $9 billion globally, according to Fairtrade International, currently the largest fair-trade organization in the world.[9] But this growth included many players who did not share the justice-for-small-farmers orientation of original fair traders. Episcopal priest and analyst David Mesenbring observes that "Christians can be rightfully credited with helping initiate and build the fair trade movement. But we are overdue in critically reviewing its evolution."[10]

Growing Pains

As a result of mainstreaming, a fair-trade advocate from 1988 would hardly recognize today's fair-trade industry. The national Max Havelaar label has given way to multiple certifications operating globally, many of which have similar-sounding names but different understandings of fair trade. Some certifiers work only with farmer cooperatives, while others contract with plantations. Many, but not all, require a minimum price for farmers. Some certifiers are independent, while others are set up and controlled by corporations, including Nestlé, Starbucks, Cargill, and McDonalds.[11] Some companies commit only to the minimum level of purchases needed to be certified fair trade (for example, 20 percent of their coffee sales), a practice known as fairwashing, while others are committed to 100 percent certified fair trade.[12]

9. https://www.fairtrade.net/impact/global-sales-overview.
10. David Mesenbring, "What Does a Fair Trade Logo Actually Mean?" *Christian Century*, December 5, 2019, www.christiancentury.org.
11. Samanth Subramanian, "Is Fair Trade Finished?" *The Guardian*, July 23, 2019, https://www.theguardian.com.
12. Daniel Jaffee and Phil Howard, "Visualizing Fair Trade Coffee,"

In other words, fair trade means different things to different actors. The original inspiration—ensuring that farmers have access to global markets as an entrée to a better life—has morphed into bare-knuckles competition for the purchasing power of well-intentioned consumers, most of whom are hard pressed to understand which labels denote a fair shake for farmers. Only the most informed activist shopper can articulate the difference between Fairtrade International, Fair Trade USA, Fair for Life, and the Small Producers' Symbol—just a few of the fair-trade labels in the market today.

THE TWO WORLDS OF FAIR TRADE

The fair-trade industry can be divided into mainstream players, on the one hand, and a small set of players known as Alternative Trade Organizations (ATOs), on the other. ATOs are the keepers of the original fair trade vision of relationship-based commerce that advances the field's original values of democracy, solidarity, and justice. ATOs include Mary O'Brien's go-to coffee company, Equal Exchange, as well as other small producers in a group called Cooperative Coffees. They include importers, roasters, and various other players in the supply chain, along with the industry group, Fair Trade Federation. They are often supported by faith groups such as Catholic Relief Services, Presbyterian Church (USA), the Unitarian Universalist Service Committee, the United Church of Christ, and the United Methodist Committee on Relief.[13] Solidarity is

---

Philip H. Howard, December 7, 2016, https://philhoward.net.

13. Catholic Relief Services and Presbyterian Church of the United States sponsored the Fair Trade Futures conference in 2010. Phyllis Robinson, "Join Us for the Fair Trade Futures Conference in Quincy, MA, Sept 2010," https://smallfarmersbigchange.coop; and Lutheran World service was involved in the 2005 conference.

the ATOs' mantra; when many ATOs were struggling to survive a decade ago, Equal Exchange invested in, and ultimately saved, sister companies such as Oke USA, a fair-trade produce company, and Equal Exchange UK, simply because they represented a values-rich alternative to traditional commerce. "We have created an ecosystem of ATOs that walk their own path, but learn together and reinforce each other," explains an Equal Exchange blog posting.[14]

In contrast to ATOs, mainstream fair-trade players are content to work in conventional global markets. Such markets feature commodified products; competition for market share; buyers and sellers as distant, anonymous actors; and differential power among actors, based on market share. It is not always clear how well small farmers fare when their output is sold in conventional markets. Mainstream fair trade has been described by Rink Dickinson, the executive director of Equal Exchange, as a place where companies, which run the gamut from well intentioned to cynical, deliver some variant of fair trade—"sometimes weak, sometimes real, and sometimes fake."[15] He refers to their offerings as "fairish trade" products.[16] As his description suggests, evaluating individual players in the conflicted-values world of mainstream fair trade is difficult and riddled with uncertainty.

A good resource for evaluating the various groups involved in fair trade is the updated *International Guide to Fair Trade Labels* put out by Fair World Project. It uses a comprehensive set of criteria to evaluate various fair-trade labels. It is exhaustive at 124 pages, but its one-page cheat sheet focuses on the key players. A standout is the Small Producers' Symbol (SPP, for its

14. Rink Dickinson "Building an Alternative Trade Organization for 2020," Equal Exchange blog, May 1, 2020, https://blog.equalexchange.coop.

15. Rink Dickinson, "Fair Trade without Fair Traders," Equal Exchange blog, February 6, 2018, https://blog.equalexchange.coop.

16. Dickinson, "Fair Trade without Fair Traders."

acronym in Spanish), the first label controlled by producers in the Global South.

DAVID IN A GOLIATH WORLD

The ATO fair-trade movement is small and outgunned, with just a tiny share of the $9 billion in global sales that the fair-trade industry generates. But it is faithful to the original vision of fair trade, and it has heart. With the continued support of people of faith and values-driven consumers, the hope is for continued growth in sales of fairly traded products from authentic fair-trade organizations that have a solid track record. In the case of coffee, this could help to reduce the glut of certified coffee in the market and direct more revenues to small farmers.

Equal Exchange's buying clubs are a way to invigorate the fair-trade movement. For more than two decades the firm has helped congregations to purchase fair-trade goods—for congregational coffee hours, as holiday gifts, and to community members for consumption at home. Now communities can expand their bulk purchases and do so with new purpose. Communities that once participated as a gesture of assistance to poor producers might participate with renewed vigor as an expression, in union with congregations across the country, of a commitment to cooperatives and a new model of economic relations.

Indeed, Equal Exchange is helping its customers to rethink their role in fair trade, inviting them to become "citizen consumers." The firm is asking its citizen consumers to play one or more of three roles: supporter/activists, drinkers/eaters of Equal Exchange products, or financial stakeholders.[17] As former co-

17. "Join Our Citizen-Consumer Community," https://equalexchange. coop.

president Rob Everts explained in a 2019 Equal Exchange podcast:

> We want to engage with actually hundreds of thousands of people around the country . . . in their whole political beings as citizen consumers, not just, you know, "how can I help buy her stuff?" . . . we're actually inviting citizen consumers people into our market-based organization . . . to play an extremely important role, ultimately possibly a governance role with a form of membership in this cooperative, that they are influencing decisions that we make, perhaps some day on the board of directors.[18]

In fact, Equal Exchange elected its first two citizen consumers to its board of directors in 2020.[19] The organization's moves are consistent with the views of the Dutch Jesuit Frans Van der Hoff, co-creator of the first certified fair-trade coffee, who noted in a 2015 video that "Fair Trade is a political movement," not just another market transaction.[20] "It is a political movement to change the rule of the market."[21]

Like the farmer groups it works with, Equal Exchange is a worker cooperative that shares profits across the company. The pay ratio between the highest- and lowest-paid Equal Exchange employees was 4:1 in 2018, a sharp contrast to the 361:1 ratio

---

18. Rob Everts, "Episode 7: Organizing for the Long Haul, blog.equal exchange.coop."

19. Susan Sklar, Manager, Interfaith Team, Equal Exchange, communication with author, June 25, 2020.

20. World Fair Trade Organization, "A Critical Look at Fair Trade by Van der Hoff Boersma," YouTube video, May 28, 2015, https://www.youtube.com.

21. World Fair Trade Organization, "A Critical Look at Fair Trade."

that prevails in the United States.[22] It is serious about creating a world of greater solidarity, a value of great interest to many faith leaders. Among its notable successes is its Coffee Congo Project, which brought Congolese coffee to the United States; sales revenues were used to help the Panzi Foundation in Congo in its work with women victims of sexual violence. Associated with the foundation is Dr. Denis Mukwege, winner of the 2018 Nobel Peace Prize for his work in combatting sexual violence.

2. Cooperatives: More than a Century of Catholic Interest

A cooperative is an enterprise owned and run by and for its members (who might be workers, consumers, producers, purchasers or other owners). Cooperatives have been of interest to Catholic leaders for more than a century. They are governed democratically; each member has the same voting power, no matter their investment in the enterprise. Cooperatives put economics in service to humanity, rather than the other way around.

A series of church leaders has lauded cooperatives as alternative economic structures that help to create lives of dignity. The first credit union in the United States, a cooperative called St. Mary's Bank in New Hampshire, was founded in 1908 by Monsignor Pierre Hevey for mill workers in the region. Another priest, Fr. José Maria Arizmendiarrieta, founded a worker cooperative in Mondragón, Spain, in 1956 that grew into the largest cooperative in the world, with more than 70,000 employees in its far-flung operations. And Spiritan Fr. Albert McKnight promoted cooperatives in the southern United States in the late-twentieth century as a vehicle for economic dignity for African Americans in particular. Many popes have been strong supporters as well, including Pope Francis, who has gone out of his way to praise worker cooperatives. Today, the Catholic Campaign for Human Development provides support for cooperatives in

---

22. Equal Exchange, "Why Equal Exchange?" https://equalexchange. coop.

the United States, while Caritas Internationalis does the same for cooperatives in a wide array of countries.

Beyond establishing themselves as cooperatives (such as credit unions; see chapter 11) faith-based institutions can promote cooperatives by serving as anchoring institutions that contract with local cooperatives for goods and services. Catholic hospitals have played this role in some cities, helping to create a co-op infrastructure that boosts cooperatives in the region.

What might new norms for ethical trade look like? They would encompass at least three dimensions: changing the terms of trade; broadening the ownership base; and giving workers a voice in business.[23]

Regarding terms of trade, the new norms would create an environment of collaboration among producers rather than cut-throat competition by creating fair pricing, long-term relationships, and risk sharing. A broadened ownership base could involve farmer cooperatives becoming more involved in the processing of coffee. Many are already milling their coffee, and some are venturing into roasting. If these functions become more widespread and if trading and marketing were added to co-op functions, the co-op would eliminate middle men and capture more of the value added across the supply chain.[24] Consumers could also be confident that their purchases are empowering farmer cooperatives rather than corporations. Finally, giving workers a voice in business refers to economic democracy, or one worker one vote, and is most often found in worker co-ops. In such businesses profit is distributed not just to investors but also to workers—a shift that could provide a structural check on inequality.

23. Ed Mayo and Erinch Sahan, "Can We Have a Fair Trade Economy?" Coop News, May 11, 2018, https://www.thenews.coop.
24. Roozen, "Organizing Hope."

The leap from passive purchaser to citizen consumer is huge. But the reward could be huge, too, if it helps authentic fair trade to take root and grow. It may be the kind of shift needed for people of faith to realize our full potential as justice-oriented consumers. From individual to community member, from consumer to activist, from market taker to market shaper: imagine these as consumption norms in your faith community.

LEAVENINGS

The added value that faith groups can bring to fair trade is to preserve and expand the original vision of the movement: to help farmers and craftspeople earn a just wage for their work. Interest in a fair shake for poor producers is evident: global sales are robust, and now entire towns are ensuring that a critical percentage of their sales are certified by third-party certification schemes. But this interest is too often captured by fair-trade players who are not committed to the original vision of the movement.

Churches, synagogues, and other houses of worship understand the joy that comes from direct commerce with struggling producers, and the dignity and justice it can afford those producers. Taking fair trade to the next level—strengthening relationships and expanding the relational model to a wider range of producers and consumers, and thereby strengthening solidarity commerce—would benefit not only struggling producers but could be an inspiration for creating fairer economies. Indeed, innovations from the solidarity economy toolbox might apply here, from barter clubs and time banks (where hours of service are credited and redeemable for services for oneself) to "free stores" such as food pantries. Such innovations may be easily applied at the parish level and could serve as models of justice that influence the broad outlines of larger economies.

RESOURCES

Equal Exchange—a leader among alternative trade organizations, Equal Exchange sells fair trade coffee, chocolate, and other items, https://equalexchange.coop.

Fair World Project—a trade group that promotes alternative trade and publishes the International Guide to Fair Trade Labels, https://fairworldproject.org.

Faith-led Fair Trade—Catholic Relief Services, Presbyterian Church (USA), the Unitarian Universalist Service Committee, the United Church of Christ, and the United Methodist Committee on Relief partner with Equal Exchange in fair trade, https://equalexchange.coop/ee-and-you/congregations.

Ten Thousand Villages and SERRV—pioneers in fair trade, still in business today, www.tenthousandvillages.com and www.serrv.org.

11

Local Finance

In the early 2000s, "Maria," a woman in Arlington, Virginia, was in a fix. Pressed for cash, she took out a $2,000 "car title loan," a short-term advance that used her car as collateral. But Maria could not pay off the loan within its thirty-day term and instead took out a second advance to pay off the first, racking up more fees and interest in what might have become a downward spiral of debt. Soon Maria was paying 300 percent *per month*—$500 in *interest alone* each month. Such loans are rightly called "predatory," because they target people on the economic margins who are at high risk of falling into a debt trap.[1]

Maria needed help. Her situation came to the attention of Dan Morrisey, CEO and treasurer of the Queen of Peace Arlington Federal Credit Union, a parish-affiliated credit union chartered in 1964. Morrisey sprang into action, registering Maria in Our Lady Queen of Peace parish so that she could qualify for credit union membership. He quickly approved a loan of $2,500, then walked Maria to her lender to pay off the predatory note, putting an end to the financial hemorrhaging.

The Queen of Peace loan was a godsend: Maria's new interest rate at the parish credit union was far lower than that of

1. Dan Morrisey, communication with author, February 20, 2020.

the predatory loan, about 9 percent *annually*. The parish credit union charged her less in total interest over the two-year term of the loan than she paid in just one month to the predatory lender. Indisputably, the tiny parish credit union, with net assets of just $2.4 million—about 1 percent the size of the average credit union in the United States—made an enormous difference to Maria's well-being and in her prospects moving forward. Morrisey notes with pride that Maria's story is one of many in which parishioners living on the financial edge found a greater measure of economic security because of the parish's commitment to an economics of solidarity and justice.

Who knew that a house of worship could have its own credit union? Since when can capital be pooled at the neighborhood level, under the management of neighbors, and be used to benefit neighbors? How often does the CEO of a financial institution walk with a client to make a critical payment? Might faith-based credit unions play a greater role in providing financial justice for people living on the economic margins?

Morrisey's inspirational story offers hope that grassroots economics can help to seed communities of justice and opportunity. But despite the just outcome for Maria, the story has a worrisome epilogue. After more than half a century of successful operations, the Queen of Peace Federal Credit Union was absorbed into a larger, secular one in 2017, succumbing, like many other small credit unions, to regulatory and technological requirements that proved too burdensome. Indeed, faith-inspired credit unions across the United States are struggling to remain viable precisely when local capital formation is becoming more important than ever as climate and sustainability crises wreak havoc on local communities. Can the faith model of finance survive, and even thrive, when it may be needed most?

What Is a Credit Union?

At first glance, credit unions may seem little different from banks. Each offers savings and checking accounts, home and business loans, and in many cases, access to ATMs and online banking. But differences between the two institutional types are real and important:

Profits. Banks are for-profit corporations that distribute their profits to stockholders. Credit unions are not-for-profit cooperatives; profits are returned to member-owners, typically in the form of better rates and fewer fees.[2] Like all not-for-profits, credit unions do not pay corporate taxes (although they do pay employment and other taxes), which helps them to maintain lower fees.

Roots. Large banks are often distant from their customers, but credit unions, along with many community banks, are typically locally grounded; they stimulate local economies by circulating capital and increasing economic activity within a city or region. They also support community projects, sometimes by providing funding for local charities.

Size. In 2016, assets of the average U.S. bank were nearly fourteen times larger than assets held by the average credit union.[3] Indeed, credit unions can be quite small, as the $2.4 million Queen of Peace Arlington Federal Credit Union suggests. Small credit unions sometimes offer more personalized ser-

---

2. NCUA, "Comparison of Average Savings, Deposits and Loan Rates at Credit Unions (CUs) and Banks: For December 27, 2019," https://www.ncua.gov.

3. Economics and Statistics Department, "Frequently Requested U.S. Credit Union/Commercial Bank Comparisons," spreadsheet at Credit Union National Association, https://www.cuna.org.

vice, but usually they also offer a narrower range of services and, in some cases, may be more financially fragile.

Membership. Banks serve the general public, but a credit union has a defined "field of membership"; a set of common interests such as a common employer, shared geography, or membership in a group, such as a union or faith group. There are also federal credit unions, with broader and less exclusive memberships.[4]

Credit unions are more popular than ever in the United States, but there are fewer players. Credit union membership grew by a third between 2010 and 2019, while the number of institutions fell by 30 percent.[5] The consolidation trend is expected to continue; the number of credit unions could decline by another 40 percent to fewer than 3,000 by 2030.[6] Consolidation is driven by the growing regulatory burden for administrators and customer preference for amenities like online banking, among other factors. These challenges are especially difficult for the smallest credit unions with limited fields of membership—characteristics of many faith-based credit unions.

Faith and Finance

In 2020, some 410 faith-affiliated credit unions were listed on the website of the National Credit Union Association—less than 2 percent of all credit unions in the United States, but perhaps a large number to people unaware that a faith-affiliated small

4. https://www.gobankingrates.com/banking/credit-unions/types-credit-unions/.

5. Aaron Passman, "The Credit Union Issues That Defined the Decade," *American Banker,* December 31, 2019, viewed February 11, 2020, https://www.americanbanker.com.

6. Passman, "Credit Union Issues."

finance nexus exists at all.[7] Most are Catholic, but examples from Jewish, Buddhist, and Muslim groups can also be found. Membership in faith-affiliated institutions is open to people of particular faith groups who seek to live out faith values in their financial lives.

Faith-based credit institutions in the United States go back to at least the 1880s, when Hebrew Free Loan Societies were transplanted from Eastern Europe to assist budding Jewish businesses. Similarly, Catholic missionaries brought the concept of credit unions from Italy and Germany to the United States. The first credit union in the United States, St. Mary's Bank in New Hampshire, was founded in 1908 by a parish priest who sought to help French Canadian immigrants who worked in the city's mills. And leading Catholics from Pope Pius X to St. Anthony Mary Claret, founder of the Claretian order, strongly supported credit unions. The Catholic Credit Union Association has observed that "every pope in the past 120 years has encouraged and promoted credit unions."[8] Indeed, Pope Francis has been a big promoter.

---

1. Pope Francis on Credit Unions[9]

In 2015, Pope Francis used the sixtieth anniversary of the founding of the Cooperative Credit Bank in Italy to underscore the values dimensions of credit unions that he found especially important. He exhorted the gathered credit union leaders to:

Remember the weakest—bear in mind the unemployed, and give particular attention to setting up new cooperative enterprises.

---

7. https://www.ncua.gov, "Research a Credit Union," online database.

8. "America Needs Her Catholic Credit Unions," CCUA blog, https://catholiccua.blog.

9. Pope Francis, "Address of His Holiness Pope Francis to the Personnel of the Cooperative Credit Bank of Rome," September 12, 2015, www.vatican.va.

Put people first—ensure that people, not "the god of money," are at the center of their financing activities.

Manage common goods—promote cooperative solutions for the management of common goods, preventing them from becoming "the property of a few or the object of speculation."

Keep money in perspective—use financial power to ensure that money is used "for solidarity and for society" and that "capital does not command over men, but men over capital."

Create an economy of honesty—remember this overarching goal of the work.

Make it global—promote the globalization of credit unions, as a way to globalize solidarity.

In sum, Francis stated that a credit union should link efficiency with solidarity, thereby working to humanize the economy.

As the century unfolded, many regions saw Catholic parishes, schools, and credit unions working collaboratively to serve Catholics' souls, minds, and bodies.[10] The relationship was bolstered by Catholic Social Teaching, with its strong economic justice emphasis, and by institutional support, for example, from a committee of bishops at the National Catholic Welfare Council.[11] Consequently, by 1960, more than eight hundred Catholic credit unions were spread across the United States. Today, however, the ranks of Catholic credit unions have shrunk to fewer than one hundred, following the trend of consolidation in the larger credit union industry.

10. Robert Kloska, communication with author, February 17, 2020.

11. Nathan DiCamillo, "Bound by Faith and Thrift: The Double-edged Sword of Christian CUs," *American Banker*, March 30, 2018, https://www.americanbanker.com.

A Question of Values

Faith interest in credit unions is usually driven by a desire to advance or protect particular values around finance. The generation and use of money and other assets have a strong moral component in many faith traditions, giving faith groups an interest in expressing their values in the realm of finance. These values might be divided into four categories: justice, scriptural prohibitions, mutual aid, and community assistance.

Justice Values

Some attributes of credit union principles, especially their status as not-for-profits and co-ops, and their care for local communities, evoke many faith values in the broadest sense, and often in contrast to profit maximization, the dominant ethos of private banks. Todd Sipe, president and CEO of Thrivent Federal Credit Union, sees credit unions as offering a different kind of economy. "There has to be a better path than consumerism and overbuying and overspending to the point where it's tough to live a life of contentment and generosity," he observes.[12] Similarly, Bob Sutherland of Shambhala Federal Credit Union, a Buddhist-centered institution, sees credit unions as a moderating force for the economy. If they did not exist, he believes, the trend would be toward further monopolization of finance.

---

2. Mindful Finance for a Mindful Society

The Shambhala Credit Union in Boulder, Colorado, founded in 1975, has 355 members. It is rooted in the Shambhala community, a set of spiritual centers that follow the principles of Shambhala Buddhism, with its focus on personal and societal transformation.

---

12. DiCamillo, "Bound by Faith and Thrift."

CEO Bob Sutherland sees credit unions having a natural place in a Buddhist's life. Buddhist practice, he explains, brings together heaven, represented by meditation and clarity of mind, and Earth, comprising the artifacts of our physical environment. At a Buddhist credit union, members can harmonize Buddhist values and clarity of mind with the concrete world of money and finance.

The Buddhist concept of karma, the dynamic of cause and effect, also comes into play at Shambhala. Where one saves and borrows affects oneself and the world; the intention to commit to a credit union carries over into other areas. Members like to bank with the Shambhala credit union, Sutherland says, because of the good created when money circulates in a local community.

Scriptural Prohibitions

Faith-based credit unions can create the space to live out finance-specific faith values such as the prohibition on earning or charging interest. For example, Hebrew Free Loan Societies, which started in the nineteenth century in the United States, are based on the biblical and Talmudic concept of interest-free loans. By 1927, more than five hundred HFLSs were operating in the United States and were instrumental in launching businesses for Jewish owners denied access to loans at commercial banks. But as Jewish businesses prospered and their capital needs outstripped the capacity of HFLSs, they were increasingly served by commercial banks. Free-loan societies continue to exist today—on a small scale—and play an important role in helping people through short-term spells of financial difficulty.[13] For example, in spring 2020, the Hebrew Free Loan Society of New York sus-

---

13. Shelly Tenenbaum, "Immigrants and Capital: Jewish Loan Societies in the United States, 1880–1945," *American Jewish History* 76, no. 1 (1986): 67–77.

pended loan payment requirements because of the downturn in employment and economic activity due to COVID-19.[14]

Muslims are also prohibited, by the Qur'an, from charging interest for loans and from paying interest on deposits. Nevertheless, the Jafari No-Interest Credit Union (JNICU), a small Houston-based institution founded in 2016, offers Muslims interest-free options for accessing car loans, student loans, and eventually, mortgages. In place of high interest rates for riskier borrowers, JNICU simply sets a lower borrowing limit for them. And in lieu of interest charges, it covers annual expenses using a $3 monthly fee for all accounts, supplemented by two voluntary fees. "As long as our expenses are covered," says CEO and manager Imran Dhanji, "we are covered. We are not here to make money." One measure of its success: JNICU estimates that it has saved its borrowers some $272,000 in interest in its short history.[15] Another measure is the confidence members have in the institution, which Dhanji attributes to its nonprofit status. "When you mix the profit motive with social activity, things get messy," he explains. "People of faith have more confidence when they know they are supporting a nonprofit."[16]

MUTUAL AID VALUES

Some faith groups set up mutual aid societies to offer support within their communities. Jews establishing free credit societies in the United States were motivated, in part, by a desire to access capital that was denied to them by commercial banks.

---

14. Hebrew Free Loan Society, "Hebrew Free Loan Society Offers Two-Month Delay On All Current Loan Repayments For Borrowers, Providing $1.3 Million In Relief," Press Release, March 22, 2020, hfls.org.

15. Jafari No-Interest Credit Union, http://www.jafaricu.com/#services.

16. Imran Dhanji, conversation with author, February 22, 2020. (All quotes in this paragraph came from that interview.)

And Anabaptists—the Amish, Mennonites, Friends, and other denominations renowned for their close-knit communities—institutionalize their strong sharing values at Everence Federal Credit Union in Lancaster, Pennsylvania. It offers a MyNeighbor credit card that donates 1.5 percent of every purchase to any of nine thousand charities, and its Everence Sharing Fund provides grants, for necessities from food to heating oil, to people in need.[17] Meanwhile, Mormons face a unique financial need, the expense of self-funded mission trips. They can use the Missionary Savings Account at Beehive Federal Credit Union, a Mormon-owned institution, to help Mormon children start their mission saving early in life. The account offers a yield many times greater than the average interest rate in the country.[18]

Community Assistance

Faith-based credit unions, especially larger ones that are financially stable, often add a "giving back" component to their mission by making grants to community organizations. For example, Ohio Catholic Federal Credit Union practices the biblical principle of tithing; it dedicates 10 percent of profits to help community nonprofits, part of which involves an innovative challenge-grant program in Catholic schools built on the Parable of the Talents.

---
3. Students Live the Parable of the Talents[19]

Ohio Catholic Federal Credit Union (OCFCU) uses the Parable of the Talents from the Gospel of Matthew to educate about

---

17. https://www.everence.com.

18. Erik Payne, "How 4 Credit Unions Tie Faith to Finances," CreditUnions.com, August 1, 2020, https://www.creditunions.com.

19. Dean Robinson, mission coordinator, communication with author, February 14, 2020.

financial stewardship, charitable giving, and teamwork. Catholic school children study the parable, which tells of servants who are challenged to shepherd an investment and increase its value. Classes are given an OCFCU grant of $500 and asked to increase it over the course of several months, with the proceeds going to a nonprofit working in community service or social justice. The students develop a variety of fundraising initiatives to leverage their grant, from basketball tournaments and spaghetti dinners to theater events and sales of wristbands.

Since the program's launch in 2016, the credit union has disbursed $12,500 to schools, which the students have multiplied into $57,648 for community nonprofits. (Students can be proud of this 361 percent return, which far outstrips the 100 percent return that so pleased the master in Jesus's parable!) OCFCU Mission Coordinator Dean Robinson notes that the program "is a great evangelization method to teach them how to use their talents . . . to bring about large impact results."

Larger Catholic credit unions often have more options for giving back. The Notre Dame Federal Credit Union, the largest Catholic credit union, made approximately $4 million in profit in 2019, from which it gave back $1.2 million to its membership and the community, according to Robert Kloska, chief partnership officer. As a result, every parish in its service area that had a school and that banked with Notre Dame FCU was given $12,000 in scholarship funds. And parishes without a school received $5,000 for parish programs that help the poor.

Kloska reports other, indirect benefits emerging from the solidarity values of Notre Dame FCU. In 2010, when tellers were paid between $9.50 and $10.00 per hour, newly installed CEO Thomas Gryp set a goal: no teller should have to work a second job to make a living. So by 2020, the wage was raised to $15 per hour, a living wage in low-cost South Bend, Indiana. Similarly, paid time-off for tellers was doubled, bringing it in line with that for Notre Dame FCU executives. According to

Kloska, action on solidarity values raised the bar for all financial institutions in the area, including for banks, which also felt
pressure to increase their pay and benefits.

In sum, faith-based financial institutions have successfully
incorporated values of justice, solidarity, and the common good
into the financial lives of their members and have used accumu-
lated assets to advance particular missions. Their success raises a
question: In a world of growing inequality and regular evidence
of economic and financial injustice, can such institutions more
broadly shape finance and economics to align with faith values?

The Large and the Small of It

The simplicity of many faith-based credit unions is both their
promise and their vulnerability. In small credit unions, for
example, in a single church, participants know each other, an
intangible of great value to the credit union. It means approval
of some loans that would be denied at a bank for being too small
or too risky. Familiarity might also secure high rates of repay-
ment. The administrator at tiny St. Thomas Credit Union in
Arlington, Virginia, reports that he did not worry too much if
members fell behind in their payments because social pressure
would typically keep them faithful to their commitments. After
all, members share pews and a Communion line—social and
spiritual ties that are deeply important to them.

Still, small credit unions are at risk if they cannot keep up
with regulations—which have grown stringent, especially with
concerns over terrorist-related money laundering—and if they
are unable to offer services increasingly sought by customers.
As people embrace ATMs, online banking, a call center, and
smartphone apps, for example, credit unions run by volunteers
are hard-pressed to compete. Indeed, data from the Catholic

Credit Union Association shows that their smallest member firms found survival difficult in the five-and-a-half-year period between December 2013 and May 2019, while the largest appeared to prosper.

A more fundamental challenge for a small credit union is making loans. Credit unions earn the interest paid to depositors by lending those deposits to borrowers and charging them interest. But if demand for loans at a small parish operation is insufficient to generate the interest promised on depositors' savings, the business formula for credit union success is in jeopardy. This is the predicament of many small credit unions today.

To help address the challenge, the Catholic Credit Union Association (CCUA) was founded in 2016. It builds bridges across member organizations, and combines lending capacities in order to "finance projects of nearly any size, in any diocese, nationwide," according to Tom Gryp at the announcement of the creation of the CCUA.[20] For example, CCUA creates opportunities for credit unions, even small ones, to help finance a loan at another institution.[21] By pooling funds to finance a project, all participating institutions earn a portion of the interest payments, even the small participants, for whom the revenue stream could keep their operation viable.

Loan participation can also facilitate the financing of large projects that are beyond the capacity of a single institution to manage. An example is Notre Dame FCU's financing of the largest Hispanic Catholic radio network in the United States, a deal worth $8 million. Although NDFCU was a medium-sized credit union, with $650 million in net assets and 180 employees, the loan was too large to shoulder alone. But opening the

---

20. Notre Dame Federal Credit Union, "Creation of Catholic Credit Union Association Announced," May 18, 2020, https://notredamefcu.com.

21. Kloska, communication with author.

lending process to several smaller credit unions made the deal possible.[22]

The Future of Faith and Finance

The credit union industry is undergoing transformations that are both challenging and helpful to faith groups. Among the most evident challenges in the United States is changing demographics. Parish credit unions with aging populations may have more savers and fewer borrowers: older people are often more interested in savings accounts and less in need of auto loans and mortgages (except perhaps for reverse mortgages). Meanwhile, younger parishioners may seek larger institutions that offer tech-based services, such as banking by phone and prepaid cards.[23] Age aside, declines in church membership may mean that some churches simply have too few members to support a viable credit union or too few people with the skills and interests to run one.

At the same time, other demographic trends suggest openings for faith-based institutions. The NCUA's Strategic Plan notes that a quarter of households in the United States either have no account at a federally insured institution (the industry calls these households "unbanked") or relies on nonbank alternative financial services.[24] And less than half of African American and Hispanic households are "fully banked."[25] These are populations that still tend to be active in church life and therefore may be interested in church-based finance.

In addition, the trend toward consolidation could offer options for overcoming the disadvantages of small size at faith-

22. Kloska, communication with author.
23. NCUA, "Strategic Plan: 2018–2022," January 25, 2018, https://www.ncua.gov.
24. NCUA, "Strategic Plan: 2018–2022."
25. NCUA, "Strategic Plan: 2018–2022."

based credit unions. Merging parish-based credit unions into a diocesan institution might allow a faith-based operation to capture the benefits of a larger institution, such as ATMs and online banking, while preserving its core values. These might be complemented by local, parish-based micro-institutions that specialize in small and perhaps informal loans akin to those made by the Hebrew Free Loan Societies.

Taken together, a strategy of outreach to unbanked populations and a strategic realignment of faith-based finances to encompass larger, full-service institutions and more informal, parish-level operations might offer flexibility for financing to navigate the coming disruptions caused by climate change and other sustainability dislocations. It is an open question whether such options, had they existed, might have helped the Queen of Peace Arlington Federal Credit Union to survive.

Leavenings

Given the economic uncertainty of the decades ahead in light of climate change and other environmental disruptions, safety nets will become critical to struggling populations. Small, local safety nets like parish credit unions, while lacking the bells and whistles of their larger siblings, might nevertheless fill a niche for people on the economic margins who need small amounts of capital. In the process, they could help low-income people to escape the exploitation of pay-day loans. Meanwhile, larger faith-based credit unions could meet the need for values-based projects that might not have access to credit elsewhere. Decentralized faith management of finance could safeguard increasingly vulnerable communities from the destabilizing forces unleashed by a less resilient climate and environment.

While the focus here has been on credit unions, other financial innovations could increase community resilience as well, such as community currencies and time banks. These local initiatives can empower localities even if higher levels of government are unresponsive to people's needs.

RESOURCES

Catholic Credit Union Association—a trade group that facilitates collaboration among Catholic credit unions, https://catholiccua.blog.

Mycreditunion.gov—U.S. government website that explains how credit unions operate, https://www.mycreditunion.gov.

National Credit Union Association—a trade group that represents the interests of credit unions. Offers extensive information on credit unions, www.ncua.gov.

Oikocredit—a faith-inspired cooperative and social investor that provides capital for sustainable development in low-income nations. Capital comes from individual and organizational investors, https://www.oikocredit.coop.

Part V

Raising Voices

12

Modern Prophets

In July 2018, the Vatican marked the third anniversary of the publication of *Laudato Si'* with an international conference featuring some of the brightest minds in sustainability. UN officials, scientists from the Potsdam Institute for Climate Impact Research and the London School of Economics, theologians, cardinals leading major Vatican departments, and major NGO leaders like Bill McKibben—an all-star cast—gathered to discuss the rapidly unfolding sustainability emergency using presentations that were at once striking and sobering.

But of all the learned discourses offered over three days in the New Synod Hall, it was the prophetic one that stood out for its powerful simplicity.

As a late session wound down toward the end of the conference, a change to the program was announced. A casually dressed, brown-skinned man with longish silver hair and a weathered face made his way to the dais and around to an empty seat. He brought no script, no PowerPoint deck, no laser pointer, no satchel or backpack. Clad in a white shirt, a necklace of animal teeth framing his open collar, Angaangaq Angakkorsuaq, an indigenous elder and shaman from Greenland, rested his dignified frame into a panelist's chair. He settled in, equipped with little more than his truth, and a prayer.

These were all he needed. For seven minutes, Angakkorsuaq,

who also goes by the nickname Uncle, held the audience spell-bound with a talk that was at once deeply personal and globally relevant. It moved and challenged the audience, and, by the end, it found hope where little would seem possible. His talk is worth relating at length.

"I come from the oldest crust of Earth, that's Greenland," he begins. His family has lived there for five thousand years, "one kilometer away from the Big Ice," on land that stands as a barometer of climate change on Earth today. "When I was born," he explains, "the Big Ice . . . was on average five kilometers thick. Now it's about two kilometers thick."

Uncle speaks of the Big Ice with love—and of its melting with a profound sense of loss. "The wisdom of the ice is disappearing," he says, noting that striations of the Big Ice read like a history book, revealing storms in the Mojave Desert, volcanic eruptions in Hawai'i, even traces of ancient Rome. He longs for the Big Ice to speak to others as it has spoken to him, so that all will understand the slow-motion disaster unfolding today—and act on it.

"I just took forty spiritual leaders of the world to Greenland . . . to walk on the Big Ice . . . it was sunny. From the surface melting of the Big Ice, one river was running at more than one million liters per second." He pauses for the benefit of the non-numerate, then advances with care. "I said *more than one . . . million . . . liters . . . per second,*" before adding the coda: *"And there are more than 10,000 rivers in Greenland!"*

Uncle grows prosecutorial, his voice rising. "And all caused by you. All of you! Every one of you!" His extended arm sweeps the room of conferees before him. "You *caused* it!" He points to his head. "You *knew* it already, that there is climate change." His palm covers his heart, his voice softening. "But do you *comprehend* what you are doing? Do you have *any* idea what you are doing?"

"I believe that you have capacity to use your knowledge wisely." A slight relaxation washes over the audience, but the reprieve is short: *"But you haven't done it. . . .* When I say you haven't done it, I *really mean* that you *have . . . not . . . done it!"*

"The impact is so big. You have no idea what's coming at you. You have literally no idea."

Uncle draws a breath and begins to pivot toward his take-home message. He observes that he no longer attends many international conferences. "But then I was invited here out of the blue," he says with amazement. "It is so interesting that I meet you. You are my last hope. Really, literally, you are the last hope of Earth. . . ."

Highly respected by his community, Uncle is a "runner" for the elders. The wisdom figures have asked him to pass along a message to the conference attendees. He does.

It lands like a snowball to the face.

"'Tell them *it is now too late. No one can stop the melting of the Big Ice.'*" The verdict, so direct and bracing, cuts to the soul. Gloom is not the language of most religious conferences, and certainly not a closing message. What are attendees to do with this?

But Uncle is not finished; despair would not have the last word. Hardly skipping a beat, he completes the elders' message with a seeming nonsequitur: "'Now tell them to create hope amongst people.'"

Only a person of great spiritual depth can discern truth in such incongruous statements—"it is now too late . . . now, create hope." But Uncle is a spiritual figure who sees a spiritual path as the way forward. "The only chance you have now: stop looking at your phones and *start listening to your spirit.* That's where your beauty is. . . . "

He expresses hope for the children who will live on after us.

He says he prays that he can give his children a life worth living, in part because "Mother Earth is stunning, absolutely stunningly beautiful." His love for our planet seems to emerge from a deep inner place and is transmitted effortlessly to the audience.

Uncle closes with a prayer, as chimes signal—prophetically?—that time was up. Sitting just a stone's throw from St. Peter's Basilica, this indigenous elder closed his eyes, bowed his head slightly, and began a haunting prayer in his native language, Kalaallisut, an intonation of vowels and exhalations. Forty seconds later, his hands open and his arms encircle the space before him, as if cradling the Earth and blowing life into it. "Aho," he concludes.[1]

That day in Vatican City, Uncle bore the unmistakable markings of a prophet. He read and reported the signs of the times. He spoke truth to the assembled powerful. He drew from a deep spiritual well and challenged attendees to honor our own spiritual depths. His tone was firm but loving; he did not mince words, yet his care for the audience and for the Earth was plain. In his capacity to challenge and offer hope, Uncle skillfully wielded tools as a Hebrew prophet might. And like the prophets of old, having made his case, Uncle left us to ourselves to ponder our next moves.

SPEAKING FOR GOD

The word "prophet" comes from the Greek *prophete,* meaning "one who speaks for another."[2] A prophet speaks for God, help-

---

1. Author's recounting of the address by Angaangaq Angakkorsuaq (Uncle) at the "Saving Our Common Home and the Future of Life on Earth" International Conference on the 3rd Anniversary of *Laudato Si'*, Vatican City, July 2018.

2. John Dear, *The Beatitudes of Peace: Meditations on the Beatitudes, Peacemaking, and the Spiritual Life* (New London, CT: Twenty-Third Publications, 2016).

ing us to discern the divine signal amid the noise of daily life. Our moment-to-moment living is filled with myriad "duties, delights, and distractions," in the words of the scholar Walter Brueggemann, but prophets help us to see through our busyness "to recognize God's action breaking into our life."[3]

Father John Dear, a social and peace activist, lays out a dozen characteristics of authentic prophets. Among other things, they are fearless truth-tellers, rooted in God, who read the signs of the times and denounce prevailing societal practices, while offering hope for a future blessed with justice. By these criteria, the sustainability movement is filled with people who arguably "speak for God." Few meet all twelve of Dear's characteristics of a prophet, but their words and deeds on the critical issues of our time certainly deserve to be called prophetic.

Dear's dozen characteristics of a prophet are condensed here to five, each brought to life by contemporaries who strive to live these principles.

Prophets have their feet on the ground. The prophet scans the event horizon, interpreting the signs of the times from the perspective of biblical mandates for justice and peace. The words of daily journalism—on war, poverty, climate change, and other critical matters—are measured against the Word that grounds prophetic truth. The prophet is not fooled by public relations spin that is driven by special interests and that deviates from God's message of justice for all. The prophet simply gives us "God's take on what's happening."[4]

Bill McKibben is a longtime climate activist and among the first to explain climate change to the public. In his 1989 book, *The End of Nature,* McKibben lays out the immensity of human-

3. Walter Brueggeman, *The Prophetic Imagination,* 40th Anniversary Ed. (Minneapolis, MN: Fortress Press, 2018), 99.
4. Dear, *The Beatitudes of Peace,* 116–17.

ity's impact on the planet: "We are at the end of nature. By the end of nature I do not mean the end of the world. The rain will still fall and the sun shine, though differently than before. When I say 'nature,' I mean a certain set of human ideas about the world and our place in it." Many years later he expressed at Riverside Church a simple and eloquent statement of what we need to do. "Our goal must be to make real the Gospel, with its injunction to love our neighbors, not to drown them, not to sicken them, not to make it impossible for them to grow crops but to love them."[5]

Prophets are grounded in justice. God's inclusive love is an inspiration for the prophet, who is attuned to the least, the vulnerable, and the marginalized. The prophet always sides with the powerless and marginalized in a world that often prefers to look away, and she applies this option for the poor to systems as much as to personal comportment. A prophet, says Dear, becomes "the voice of a voiceless God."[6]

Leonardo Boff is a social critic and onetime Franciscan who understands social systems and evaluates them from the perspective of marginalized people. In *Cry of the Earth, Cry of the Poor*, a title that became the rallying cry of *Laudato Si'*, Boff connects environmental decline and social injustice at a systemic level. "The logic that exploits classes and subjects peoples to the interests of a few rich and powerful countries is the same as the logic that devastates the Earth and plunders its wealth, showing no solidarity with the rest of humankind and future generations."[7]

5. Bill McKibben, "God's Taunt," Riverside Church, April 28, 2013, https://www.youtube.com.

6. Dear, *The Beatitudes of Peace*, 116–17.

7. Leonardo Boff, *Cry of the Earth, Cry of the Poor* (Maryknoll, NY: Orbis Books, 1997), xi.

Prophets are fearless. The prophet is courageous, consistently speaking out against injustice and in favor of marginalized people, in critiques that skewer the status quo and discomfit the powerful. The prophet usually has a difficult life and is frequently at odds with authorities, who dismiss her, and even paint her as unhinged, all the more as the prophet's message begins to resonate. Often, the prophet feels banished to the margins of society.[8] Life is uncomfortable and even dangerous, and the prophet is often in trouble.

The teenage climate activist Greta Thunberg stands out among the many who could be cited for their fearlessness in advocating for sustainability. As a fifteen-year-old, Greta sat outside the Riksdag, the Swedish Parliament, entirely alone at first, on a "school strike" that eventually awakened the conscience of the world. As unlikely a hero as the biblical David, her youth and Asperger's syndrome became strengths in her climate activism. Greta appealed to students worldwide who resonated with her climate alarm and in 2019 joined her in her climate strikes. These drew media and policymakers' attention, as well as an invitation to United Nations meetings in September 2019.

There, her Asperger's helped her to tell unvarnished truths as she addressed the media and delegates in a short, emotional appeal: "People are suffering. People are dying. Entire ecosystems are collapsing. We are in the beginning of a mass extinction, and all you can talk about is money and fairytales of eternal economic growth. How dare you!" Referring to the inadequacy of the policymakers' response and reviewing the relevant data, she added, "These numbers are too uncomfortable and you are still not mature enough to tell it like it is. You are failing us!"

True to the prophetic experience, Greta's success in communicating the urgency of the climate crisis drew dismissive

8. Dear, *The Beatitudes of Peace*, 116–17.

responses from powerful figures in the media and in politics, including President Trump, who tweeted that she had anger management issues and needed to "chill."[9]

Prophets are visionaries. Despite the prophet's ready critiques, he or she is motivated by a positive, inspiring vision and communicates hope. Prophets are grounded dreamers who keep alive God's energizing vision for humanity when others have faltered. They are confident in the viability of their vision, believing that what remains at the end of the day, no matter how discouraging the events of the world, are God and God's promises. That bedrock truth is, for the prophet, rock-solid reason never to give in to despair. [10]

Dr. Vandana Shiva is an environmental, justice, and democracy activist in India. She has fought for the rights of poor farmers to control their economic destiny and against corporate powers that attempt to appropriate nature, as, for example, through the patenting of seeds. Often involved in struggles, she exudes a positive and hopeful air. In 2003, when asked how she is able to maintain this stance she replied:

> I do not allow myself to be overcome by hopelessness, no matter how tough the situation. I believe that if you just do your little bit without thinking of the bigness of what you stand against, if you turn to the enlargement of your own capacities, just that in itself creates new potential. And I've learned from the Bhagavad Gita and other teachings of our culture to detach myself from the results of what I do, because those are not in my hands. The context is not in your control, but your commit-

9. Donald Trump tweet, @realDonaldTrump December 12, 2019, https://twitter.com/realdonaldtrump/status/1205100602025545730?lang=en.

10. Dear, *The Beatitudes of Peace*, 116–17.

ment is yours to make, and you can make the deepest commitment with a total detachment about where it will take you. . . . And that combination of deep passion and deep detachment allows me always to take on the next challenge because I don't cripple myself, I don't tie myself in knots. I function like a free being. I think getting that freedom is a social duty because I think we owe it to each other not to burden each other with prescription and demands. I think what we owe each other is a celebration of life and to replace fear and hopelessness with fearlessness and joy.[11]

Finally, and most importantly, *prophets are centered on God.* A prophet is rooted in God. She is a contemplative who spends time with God's Word, searching and listening to absorb the desire of God. Prophets begin each day by grounding themselves in the divine. From this foundation, the prophet is oriented and girded for the work that needs doing.[12] Attuned to the divine agenda, the prophet "tells us who God is and what God wants," in Dear's words.[13]

Laudato Si' is a prophetic document with a firm spiritual foundation.[14] The opening line is itself a prayer—*Laudato Si', mi' Signore,* "Praise be to you, my Lord." Pope Francis also closes the encyclical with a prayer. Indeed, the entire document emerges from and looks to God, and its critique of our treatment of the Earth and the human family is made from a place

11. Sarah Ruth van Gelder and Vandana Shiva, "Earth Democracy: An Interview with Vandana Shiva," *Yes! Magazine,* January 1, 2003, www.yesmagazine.org.

12. Dear, *The Beatitudes of Peace,* 116–17.

13. Dear, *The Beatitudes of Peace,* 116–17.

14. John Bayer, "'A Voice Crying in the Desert': *Laudato si'* as Prophecy," *The Way* 54, no 4 (2015): 68.

that joins Earth, humanity, and spirit, as when he writes about environmental degradation, "God has joined us so closely to the world around us that we can feel the desertification of the soil almost as a physical ailment, and the extinction of a species as a painful disfigurement."[15]

RELIGIOUS ADVOCACY WORK

In July 2013, Pope Francis addressed young people gathered for World Youth Day in Rio de Janeiro. In outlining his hope for the outcome of World Youth Day, the pope said that he wanted the youth to make themselves heard in their dioceses: "I want the noise to go out, I want the Church to go out onto the streets!"[16] How often do today's Christian leaders exhort adherents to take to the streets? Certainly it was an unusual call from a Catholic leader. But rarely has our prophetic vocation been so important.

This call comes not a moment too soon given the urgency of the moment. Greenhouse gas emissions must be reduced radically *this decade*—and this is just one piece of the sustainability challenge. Entire systems of transportation, energy provision, agriculture, and commerce require redesign and reconfiguring. The needed overhaul is economy-wide, and requires completion within a generation, using policies that prioritize the poor. Such a monumental challenge will be met only by mobilizing entire societies. Yet in too many nations, certainly in the United States, one would hardly know that a planetary emergency is upon us.

People of faith need to put on our prophet hats and make some noise. Lifestyle change is the quiet part of our responsibility; we also need to push our neighbors, communities, legisla-

15. Pope Francis, *Laudato Si'*, no. 89.
16. Pope Francis, "Meeting with Young People from Argentina," July 25, 2013, www.vatican.va.

tures, and leaders to take rapid comprehensive action. We need to do so centered in God, reading the signs of the times, standing with the marginalized, remaining fearless, and embracing a visionary and hope-filled posture.

Advocacy by Faith Groups

Fortunately, a growing number of organizations and opportunities are available to help us respond to the prophetic call. A variety of faith groups are active in these circles and are good outlets for advocacy and activism. They are involved in a variety of activities:

Marches and protests. Faith communities participated in marches sponsored by the People's Climate Movement in 2014, 2017, and 2018. They have also been involved in the climate strikes of 2019. Various faiths and denominations often gather to march together as a single faith family. Marches demonstrate political strength and are a barometer that get the attention of politicians.

International negotiations. Faith groups are often involved in international negotiations on sustainability issues. Green-Faith and Global Catholic Climate Movement (GCCM) often have an active presence at annual United Nations' climate talks. Faith groups use the occasions to make the faith perspective known, to build their networks, and in GreenFaith's case, to train faith leaders in organizing to build a climate and environmental movement.

Signing statements and pledges. Faith groups make their clout known through the use of statements, as individual institutions and jointly with other faith groups, on various sustainability issues. Catholic Climate Covenant offers a St. Francis Pledge that allows Catholics to commit to sustainability prin-

ciples and actions. Interfaith Power and Light offers a pledge
to be a climate justice voter. And GreenFaith has organized
statements of faith leaders concerning the climate emergency.

Education. Most faith groups provide resources to help congregations understand sustainability issues from a faith perspective: Interfaith Power and Light (IPL), for example, offers
a Climate Change 101 primer; GreenFaith has a series of
topical, faith-specific resources; and Catholic Climate Covenant and GCCM have a range of educational and activist
resources.

Legislative advocacy. CCC's advocacy offers opportunities to
speak up on current legislation, with online forms that suggest language in support of particular House and Senate bills.
It also offers tools for education, including bulletin inserts,
and outreach training, for example, in writing letters to the
editor, meeting with legislators, and in doing media interviews and public speaking. National Religious Partnership
for the Environment (NRPE) brings together a coalition of
faith groups for regular monitoring of Capitol Hill legislative
activity and for lobbying members of Congress.

Community building. Many faith groups sponsor local groups
that build community and activism. GreenFaith offers
GreenFaith Circles, CCC has Creation Care Teams, and
GCCM uses Laudato Si' Circles for these purposes. These
groups are important for creating strong ties among members and are often the base from which a variety of advocacy
actions spring.

Youth mobilization. Sustainability issues are of particular interest to youth, who will live with the consequences of today's
decisions. So engaging youth is an important and often fruitful way to create a sustainability presence. CCC's Catholic
Climate Project and GCCM's Laudato Si' Generation are

well positioned to capture the energy of the people with the greatest stake in stabilizing the climate.

Rituals and prayers. IPL, CCC, and GCCM offer a wealth of spiritual resources related to climate issues. GreenFaith offers resources tailored to particular faith traditions. Although not organizing tools themselves, they are sources of spiritual sustenance that can sustain a group's advocacy efforts.

Lifestyle. Living the Change is an interfaith site organized by GreenFaith that focuses on encouraging lifestyle change. Organizations from a variety of faiths are involved. It features a dynamic website that offers resources for simpler living, including blogs and stories of change. The site allows participants to record commitments to lifestyle change in the realms of transportation, energy, and food. An excellent site for promoting individual change, it also has resources for organizing congregational action through local suppers and guided conversations that can multiply impact.

The Big Levers

The changes needed to preserve a planet that can support humanity are huge, and the time to achieve them is short. This suggests that advocacy energy should focus on big levers that can bring comprehensive change. One of these is some version of a Green New Deal (GND), a comprehensive legislative restructuring of economies to emphasize clean energy, green jobs, and a host of economic reforms that would rapidly set a new course for industrial economies. While often criticized for being overreaching, the truth is that a broad-based economic overhaul styled on a GND is needed to match the scope of the challenge. And a comprehensive approach allows for tackling multiple challenges at once, from climate stabilization and pollution reduction to employment and infrastructure overhauls. Several faith groups, including GreenFaith, CCC, and GCCM are on record as favoring a GND.

Another big lever of change is fossil-fuel divestment and investment. GCCM has helped organize Catholic institutions to divest, and GreenFaith was a founder of the SHINE initiative to steer divested funds not just to renewables but to small-scale renewables that are designed to eliminate energy poverty, which would make a major difference in the livelihoods and development prospects of poor and vulnerable people living in isolated communities. More activity on these fronts is needed as well.

The hour is late to avoid climate catastrophe and to increase the prospects of building sustainable societies. Prophetic voices encourage us to be hopeful. At this point, hope is best grounded in energetic, vocal action. Currently, our biggest need is not to design new technologies or policies; most of the required hardware and policy papers already exist. The oft-cited missing piece, political will, is created when people make noise, much as Uncle, Bill McKibben, Leonardo Boff, Greta Thunberg, Vandana Shiva, and Pope Francis have. The full-throated voices of the faithful are now required, along with trust that God will accompany us. And as we undertake this work, we would do well to heed the advice of Pope Francis: "Let us sing as we go."[17]

17. Pope Francis, *Laudato Si'*, no. 244.

13

Responding to the Cries

The innovations explored in this volume suggest that seeds of sustainability can be found within faith traditions—in our teachings; in our prayers and rituals; in our wealth, enterprises, and purchases; and on our grounds. The intent is that the innovations will spark reflection on ways people can build more just and environmentally benign economies. They are inspirations, not blueprints, and only a down payment on the mammoth effort and structural change needed to create truly just and sustainable economies and societies. We need to hear the cry of the Earth regarding the plight of oceans, forests, and our polluted skies. We need to answer the cry of the poor by adopting tools for equity and opportunity such as worker cooperatives, and for more simple and satisfying lifestyles. These and dozens of other sustainability topics and solutions are appropriate terrain for cultivation by faith communities.

The task of building sustainable societies is enormous, complex, and urgent, and cannot be completed by faith communities alone. But a methodology for thinking about the faith role in this historic activity—which "geologian" and priest Thomas Berry once called The Great Work—is to use the "see, judge, act" practice often promoted in faith circles.

See: Being in Nature to Love Nature

A great challenge for us, as citizens of the industrial era, is to learn to see nature. Sister Pat Siemen, OP, notes that "from our head up we know that our glaciers are melting, that the oceans are warming, that small island nations are disappearing—and we still continue to do the same behavior. It's as though we are anaesthetized. . . ." Our conversion challenge is to move from head to heart, to experience nature in a way that allows us to appreciate and love it. Biologist Stephen Jay Gould once said that we must forge an emotional bond between ourselves and nature, for "we will not fight to save what we do not love."[1] Saving the natural environment requires that the cry of the Earth resonates within us until it moves our hearts.

How can we learn to love nature? How do we look at the non-human created world and learn to "think with the heart"?[2] Saint Bonaventure advises starting small, with the simplest things. The Franciscan Richard Rohr interprets Bonaventure: "Love rocks and elements first, move to trees, then animals, and then humans. Angels will soon seem like a real possibility and God is then just a short leap away. It works."[3] With even the smallest things, look, notice, and be present. Be like the retreatant who returned from a contemplative walk on the farm and remarked in amazement to his director, "Cows have eyelashes!" God is everywhere, even in the smallest details, when we take time to see.

Daily walks are an easy way to incorporate nature in our daily

1. Stephen Jay Gould, "Enchanted Evening," *Natural History* 100 (1991): 4–14.

2. Ilia Delio, Keith Douglass Warner, and Pamela Wood, *Care for Creation: A Franciscan Spirituality of the Earth* (Cincinnati: Franciscan Media, 1999), 16.

3. Richard Rohr, "The Great Chain of Being," *The Mendicant*, Summer 2019.

lives. Walk with the eyes of St. Francis, seeing God expressed in every living and nonliving thing, and reflecting praise and gratitude back to God. The Global Catholic Climate Movement has created a Laudato Si' Chaplet that can spiritually enrich even an urban stroll (see below, Laudato Si' Chaplet). And of course, we can also build firsthand experiences of nature into our spiritual lives. Retreats often provide ample opportunity for interaction with nature; imagine a retreat undertaken as a camping trip for a more complete immersion in the natural environment. Liturgies and prayer services can incorporate natural elements such as water or living things, and in some cases can be held outdoors. Religious education can also foster a connection with nature, for example, by adapting a module on food and hunger to tap the magic of a church vegetable garden. To see nature, we need only look, with intention. Her "welcome sign" is everywhere; visible at every moment for those with eyes to see.

1. Laudato Si' Chaplet[4]

The Global Catholic Climate Movement has developed a creative chaplet (a form of prayer similar to the rosary) based on St. Francis's Canticle of the Creatures. The practice is meant to cultivate the spiritual dispositions of praise and universal fraternity. Each decade of the chaplet focuses on an element of nature, dubbed with the names used by St. Francis: Mother Earth, Sister Water, Brother Fire, and Sister Air. It is usually prayed outdoors—the preferred prayer locales of Jesus and St. Francis, GCCM notes.

The chaplet borrows language directly from the Canticle of the Creatures. A decade might use "Praise be you, my Lord, through your sister, Mother Earth," repeated ten times as the practitioner reflects on the Earth around her. Succeeding decades focus on other elements of nature. Bookending the

4. "Laudato Si' Chaplet," Global Catholic Climate Movement, https://ourcommonhome.org.

four decades are an opening song of praise and a reading, and at the close, the Lord's Prayer or a prayer of the Earth. The practice often includes a few minutes of quiet listening, attuned to God in the surrounding nature.[5]

The chaplet is flexible, with the option to incorporate additional elements as suggested by one's outdoor experience (for example, Sister Oak, Brother Robin). And the interpretation of an element can be varied. "Sister Air" may refer to the breeze experienced by the practitioner, or to her breath, or simply to the space between things. Brother Fire might be the sun, feelings of anger, or the metabolism in one's body. The format can also be shifted from "Praise be You" to a focus on gratitude, "Thank you, Lord, through Brother Wind . . . ," or repentance, "I am sorry, my Lord, for my abuse of Sister Water. . . ."[6] The chaplet is a rich practice for deepening the human-God-Earth relationship that Pope Francis speaks of in *Laudato Si'*.[7]

Taking Stock of Nature

As we become active, conscious observers of the natural world, we can explore our dependence on nature by undertaking a field survey of resources that we already use—food, water, electricity, and gasoline—but also waste-absorption services, such as garbage collection and sewage treatment. Each is associated with a facility that, in many cases, is open for public visits: a peri-urban farm, water treatment plant, power plant, refinery, landfill, or a sewage treatment plant. A faith group might visit one facility each month, as a focus for a resource discussion that could answer questions such as:

- Where does the resource (e.g., water, gasoline) come from, and where does the waste go?

5. "Laudato Si' Chaplet."
6. "Laudato Si' Chaplet."
7. Pope Francis, *Laudato Si'*, no. 66.

- How is the environment impacted by our use of the resource or waste-absorption service?
- Can the resource or waste-absorption service be managed more sustainably? Where would it fit in a circular economy?
- Who owns the resource? Who should own the resource?
- How much of the resource, or the waste-absorption service, is locally supplied?
- What would be the impact if this resource were to disappear tomorrow?
- Do low-income people have access to the resource?
- Are low-income people disproportionately exposed to waste collection, for example, by living near a landfill or power plant?
- How should we view the resource from a spiritual perspective?
- How can our faith community be involved in making each facility more sustainable?

Prayerful appreciation of the systems that support us can remove the illusion of autonomy from nature that afflicts many in industrial societies. It can also engender a sense of gratitude for these systems and teach us how to make them greener. We might experience a conversion from being oblivious consumers to conscious ones, deepening the ecological component of our spirituality. We might also develop ways to pray about the gifts given to us by God in nature (see below, 2. Unitarian Universalists Water Communion), and we might build community as we undertake these activities as a faith group and also in partnership with other faith communities.

---

2. Unitarian Universalists Water Communion

Unitarian Universalists (UUs) hold an annual water service, sometimes called a "water communion" or "Waters of the World." It is a ritual that marks the start of a new church year each fall, when members have returned from summer travels.

Members bring samples of water from near and far and com-
mingle them in a large bowl in a ritual that signifies oneness out
of many.[8] Sometimes the water is kept, purified, and used later
as sacred water in congregational events such as child dedication ceremonies.[9]

With a fresh appreciation of God's support of us through the
gifts of nature, a logical next step is to undertake an internal
audit that documents our use of those gifts. Audits of a parish
or family can be done simply by analyzing a year's worth of
bills for each resource to establish annual and seasonal baselines
that are helpful in measuring progress in lowering one's resource
footprint. These can be compared to average use for the region
or city, and to sustainable consumption levels. Alternatively, an
ecological footprint calculator can be used to determine one's
overall use of biological resources and to compare the results
against sustainable levels to determine our extent of "ecological
deficit"—using more than the per-capita availability of biological resources—and to compare our footprint against the average
footprints of people in other countries.

Another helpful method for seeing nature is to use a creative exercise developed by Joanna Macy, a renowned Buddhist
ecologist, called the Council of All Beings. Ideal for a parish
retreat day or some other event that allows for reflection and
discussion, the exercise asks participants to step into the shoes
of some part of nature: an owl, a river, a farm field, a rock, or
some other element, biological or not, animate or not. Participants spend time contemplating the lived reality of their chosen
element, prompted by questions from a facilitator. Then each

8. "Water Rituals and Ingatherings, Revitalized," Harvard Square
Library, https://www.harvardsquarelibrary.org.

9. "Celebrating the Water Communion," Unitarian Universalist Association, https://www.uua.org.

person makes a mask that depicts the persona of the element they have become. Finally, a Council of All Beings is called, at which participants gather in a circle to present themselves, in character, to the assembled. They describe themselves, how they live, and what is happening to them today. Each concludes, still in character, by sharing with the council a piece of wisdom that emerges from its experience.[10] Participants often report a deep sense of connection with the natural world. Entered into prayerfully, the exercise can have profound spiritual significance.

We might see nature institutionally by supporting legal codes that protect nature. In *Laudato Si'*, Pope Francis speaks lovingly of the Earth Charter, the globally endorsed statement that declares that "protection of Earth's vitality, diversity, and beauty is a sacred trust."[11] And in 2015, Pope Francis declared that "a true 'right of the environment' does exist" in part because humanity is part of the environment but also because "every creature, particularly a living creature, has an intrinsic value, in its existence, its life, its beauty and its interdependence with other creatures."[12] Seeing nature may involve becoming familiar with advances in this area. The Community Environmental Legal Defense Fund (CELDF) lists more than thirty-nine substantive initiatives at the local, tribal, national, and even international level that have advanced the rights of nature since 2001. More than a third have emerged in 2018 and 2019, suggesting that efforts may be accelerating. One is the Universal Declaration of the Rights of

10. Institute for Humane Education, "Council of All Beings," https://humaneeducation.org.

11. Pope Francis, *Laudato Si'*, no. 207; See also Klaus Bosselmann and J. Ronald Engel, *The Earth Charter: A Framework for Global Governance* (Amsterdam: KIT Publishers, 2010).

12. Pope Francis, "Meeting with the Members of the General Assembly of the United Nations Organization," United Nations Headquarters, New York, September 25, 2015, www.vatican.va.

Mother Earth, adopted in 2010, that affords explicit rights to the natural world, much as rights have been expanded to others once marginalized, including women, slaves, and indigenous peoples over recent decades and centuries.

Seeing the Marginalized Person

In *Laudato Si'*, Pope Francis writes that humanity tends to hold "little clear awareness of the problems that affect the excluded. Yet they are the majority of the planet's population, billions of people."[13] We are all too skilled at overlooking what is inconvenient to see. And even when the data penetrates, its scandalous character often does not. Consider that two thousand billionaires hold as much wealth as the world's poorest 4.6 billion people, according to Oxfam.[14] Eyebrows are raised, but not voices. Oxfam tries a different tack: if you saved $10,000 every day since Egypt's pyramids were built, you would have only a fifth of the average wealth of today's top five billionaires.[15] Silence. These realities, unacceptable in any moral universe that most of us would construct, fail to spur us to act.

Yet our consciousness is penetrable. In 2020, many white Americans experienced a deep transformation as they saw the suffering of African Americans in entirely new ways. The murder of George Floyd at the hands of a white officer in Minneapolis, the cumulative impact of cell phone videos of police violence against African Americans, and black voices that awakened white America to realities previously unseen, though in plain sight, seemed to awaken white America at a depth unknown in the history of the United States. This seeming conversion

13. Pope Francis, *Laudato Si'*, no. 49.
14. Max Lawson et al., "Time to Care," Oxfam International, January 20, 2020, https://www.oxfam.org.
15. Lawson et al., "Time to Care."

moment for much of white America, born of experience, is the transformative seeing needed to understand poverty in our country and our world.

Indeed, the key word is experience. It is commonplace to hear the expression, "To understand the poor we must walk with the poor." We do not truly see poor people, or any people, from a distance. Understanding the plight and needs of low-income people requires knowing their neighborhoods and hearing their stories directly. It requires relationship; something that congregations understand. Faith communities offer the chance for encounter at soup kitchens, homeless shelters, unemployment groups, and a multitude of other places. Encounter changes hearts. Through encounter, we read data, like that of Oxfam International or poverty data from the government, and begin to make judgments.

JUDGE: ASSESS THE REALITY

The first chapter made the case that human activities are badly degrading the planet; those facts need not be repeated here. To assess the planet's environmental situation from a moral perspective requires simply rereading the chapter while standing in the shoes of Saints Francis and Bonaventure, Teilhard de Chardin, and Thomas Berry. Their perspectives should highlight our fundamental error: treating the Earth as a warehouse for human activity rather than as a gift that we embrace with gratitude and mutuality. We can surely make the judgment that economies that overtax the resource base by overcutting forests, overpumping aquifers, and the like, or overwhelm nature's waste absorption capacity, represent a destructive posture vis-à-vis creation. And where greed and spiritual emptiness are driving this behavior, we can identify root causes that people of faith are equipped to help fix.

Meanwhile, our current economies are often deficient in providing for all people. This is not the place to lay out an alternative economic vision, but as a starting point, we can surely agree that any economy we build should align with our values. Economist Jeffrey Sachs of Columbia University reminds us that, for the ancient Greeks, economies were essentially moral endeavors whose purpose was to help create well-being. Only much later, in the sixteenth century, did the goal of well-being morph into wealth maximization with the advent of capitalism, which celebrated self-interest as an economic driver and viewed nature as a set of resources for exploitation, creating inequality and degradation.

Faith groups agree that economies, at their core, are essentially moral endeavors. Consider the 1996 "Framework for Economic Life" from the U.S. Catholic bishops. Five of the ten principles in the framework contain the word "moral"—for example, "a fundamental *moral* measure of any economy is how the poor and vulnerable are faring"—and the other principles are loaded with moral content without using the word. Yet, a quick scan of the framework reveals two clear truths: (1) the principles set high standards for ensuring that the economy is in fact moral, and (2) the U.S. economy falls woefully short of the standards. The U.S. economy fails to meet basic needs for all, provide just wages for all, and ensure that the poor are faring well, to name a few of its moral shortcomings.

A large gap exists between the powerful visions of people of faith, in this case, Catholic leadership, and the reality on the ground. This is fertile terrain for people of faith to plow. Indeed, imagine Catholics insisting that the Framework for Economic Life and similar visionary documents become *lived* principles, similar to the Amish insistence on following their values, as illustrated in chapter 7. The United States would have a fundamentally different economic order—one that is more just and more reflective of human dignity.

ACT: HANDS-ON ENGAGEMENT

Noteworthy examples of faith commitment to building sustainable societies are now apparent. At the international level, the Parliament of the World's Religions and the World Council of Churches have, for years, issued challenges to their members and adherents regarding the need to care for the environment, as have globally focused religious NGOs such as GreenFaith, Religions for Peace, and the Global Catholic Climate Movement. And the Vatican's seven-year program to build a mass movement in favor of "total sustainability," an all-hands-on-deck initiative, has the potential to bear great fruit. The Laudato Si' Action Platform challenges families, dioceses, schools, universities, hospitals, businesses, and religious orders to demonstrate commitments on a range of sustainability actions, from adoption of renewable energy to simplified lifestyles, and development of ecological catechesis, retreats, and prayer.[16] The aim is to build, over time, nothing less than a faith-led mass movement in the spirit of *Laudato Si'*. Each of these international efforts offers numerous opportunities for involvement.

National Level

National church institutions can potentially activate large numbers of members across their networks on behalf of sustainability. A program worth highlighting because of its rapid growth and because its model is easily replicable is an inspiring ecumenical movement in France called Église Verte (Green

---

16. Dicastery for Promoting Integral Human Development, "*Laudato Si'* Special Anniversary Year," http://www.humandevelopment.va.

Church) that emerged in 2017 to help churches across France make sustainability commitments. The program is a joint effort of the French Protestant Federation, the Catholic Conference of Bishops, the Assembly of Orthodox Bishops in France, and the broader Christian Council of Churches in France. It grew out of the churches' commitments emerging from the Twenty-first Conference of the Parties (COP21) and the Paris Agreement, and has struck a chord: after just three years, the movement had grown to 490 member communities across France.

Église Verte uses a five-part structure to shepherd communities to greater levels of commitment. ("Communities" denotes not just congregations but other faith-related groups including retreat centers, hospitals, schools, monasteries, and convents.) Commitment is measured using a comprehensive diagnostic tool with dozens of questions covering services and catechesis, buildings, land, local and global engagement, and lifestyles. Questions explore a broad range of activity, from whether creation is a prayer topic for the community, to the inclusion of environmental issues as part of adult education, to whether the community encourages walking and biking.

Scores from the diagnostic tool place a community in one of five categories, named for various natural elements cited in the Bible. Taken together, they suggest progression and growth, from the entry-level "Mustard Seed" designation to the "Cedar of Lebanon" label, denoting very strong environmental commitment.[17] The idea is not to encourage competition among communities, explains Laura Morosini of Église Verte, but to encourage participation—about a third of the member communities are at the entry level—and to advance from there.[18]

17. Laura Morosini, Église Verte, December 9, 2019.

18. Morosini, Église Verte, December 9, 2019. The tool is available in French on the Église Verte website and can be easily translated.

Participants report that Église Verte has made a difference in their community. Anne-Sophie Serrurier, a parishioner at St. Gabriel parish in Paris, reports that her parish proposed taking on a composting project. They set up a composting area in the garden next to the church, which opens thirty minutes before Mass. People bring discards from home and add them to the compost center, discussing with others their practices and lessons learned. Anne-Sophie tells of one participant who was heavily involved in zero-waste activities in Paris but has not been an active member of the church. The composting area drew him not just to composting but back into the parish as well. She concludes that "young people are realizing how much we need to change our lives, and that the church has something to offer."[19] Indeed, young people, who have such a great stake in how economies and societies are shaped in the decades ahead, are a rich area of interest for faith-driven sustainability advocates.

3. Creative Approaches for Appealing to Youth

The Federation of Protestant Youth in Germany (AEJ), which represents thirty-four national Protestant groups, has pursued justice and peace issues since its founding in 1948. In recent years, it has engaged on sustainability issues as well—in part because of the topic's salience for youth. It has encouraged the purchase of fair-trade products, and in November 2019, it passed a major resolution calling for social-ecological transformation. This was an important political signal that all Protestant youth have spoken with one voice, and a sign of hope.

AEJ has developed creative approaches to education on sustainability issues that are designed to appeal to young people. It has developed a game called The World in the Kaleidoscope that challenges players to address daily life decisions that involve competing values, such as weighing concern about

19. Anne-Sophie Serrurier, conversation with author, December 12, 2019.

the climate against the reality that a short-haul flight may be cheaper than a more climate friendly train ticket. The game is not meant to give "right" and "wrong" solutions to dilemmas but rather foster discussion in a search for creative solutions.

AEJ is also working to develop a multimedia Bible tool, designed to highlight parts of the Bible that speak about creation, migration, justice, food and nutrition, and other topics of social and environmental interest. It might also highlight biblical passages that teach the concept of limitations—the idea, important for sustainability, that as humans we grow and mature most under a set of constraints or limitations, an important counterpoint to the incessant "you can have it all" message that often dominates advertising today.

Parish Level

A growing number of parish and congregational groups are taking on environmental issues through "creation care" and similar committees. These laudable efforts suggest that issues of nature and the environment increasingly matter at the grassroots faith level. Still, many such groups lack the sense of urgency and comprehensiveness that a sustainability response demands and that *Laudato Si'* calls for. And many seem to capture only the few members of congregations interested in environmental issues with little relationship to the fuller faith community of which they are a part.

A notable exception is St. John Neumann parish in Reston, Virginia. Its Care for Our Common Home (CCH) ministry has grown rapidly since its creation in 2015 following the release of *Laudato Si'*. Key to its success is the committee's grasp of the broad and integrated nature of creation care. The breadth of CCH activity at St. John Neumann is evident in their dizzying variety of initiatives, organized around spirituality, education, sustainability, and advocacy. These activities range from outdoor prayer walks and presentations on waste reduction to roadside trash collection and marching for climate action (see Table F). The committee is studying ways to help parishioners convert to wind and solar power at home and is saving funds for rooftop solar panels when the church roof is replaced in a few years.[20] The dozens of initiatives at the church were undertaken in just five years, indicating the importance committee members and the entire parish assign to the ministry.

F. Select CCH Activities at St. John Neumann Parish, 2015–2020[21]

Area of Interest	Activity
Spirituality	• purchase and dedication of a St. Francis of Assisi garden statue • installation of six prayer pillars, creating a prayer loop on church grounds • Lenten presentation on *Laudato Si'* for parish families • tree planting, blessing, and prayer service on Earth Day • special liturgy to mark the World Day of Prayer for the Care of Creation • annual Blessing of the Animals • hosting outdoor prayer walks • adapting the monthly parish prayer vigil for peace, life, and justice for use in the Season of Creation • praying a virtual rosary focused on *Laudato Si'*

20. Robert More, Ed Sabo, and Janet Broderick, CCH members at St. John Neumann parish, Reston, VA, conversation with author, May 4, 2020.
21. http://cfoch.weebly.com.

Education	• hosting a film and discussion on consumerism • presenting videos by Franciscan Fr. Daniel P. Horan on *Laudato Si'* • presentation on natural burials • discussion of how to talk about climate change • parish care for creation showcase covering spirituality, Catholic Social Teaching, energy saving, and advocacy • presentation on the environmental and social aspects of clothes manufacturing	• presentation on electronic waste • showcase on food choices for personal and planetary health • youth photo contest • presentation on skin care and cleaning products • hosting a tree identification walk • participating in interfaith creation care showcase
Sustainability	• quantifying savings from parish energy efficiency measures • bird-watching walks • creation and maintenance of a pollinator garden • quarterly roadside trash pickups • planning for net-zero CO2 emissions	• touring a nearby recycling facility • hosting fair-trade sales featuring organic products • hosting a weekly farmers' market featuring organic produce • arranging for composting of food scraps from parish social events
Advocacy	• participating in People's Climate March and Catholic Climate Lobby Day • lobbying federal, state, and local officials • engaging parish children to write to Pope Francis	• letter from the pastor to the governor on clean power initiatives • presentation on Advocacy 101 • inviting a talk from a state delegate

The CCH committee takes care to mesh with other parish ministries. "One of the ways we will know we've been successful is if we integrate care for creation into all of our ministries," observes committee member Janet Broderick.[22] Members have prepared curricula on care for creation for religious education classes at the parish. They host regular outreach and educational events to include the larger parish community in their work. And in an impressive gesture of humility, they offer to wash dishes at parish events run by other ministries—for example, at the winter hypothermia shelter—so those ministries avoid using disposable dishware at their events.[23]

Importantly, the group is also integrated into the parish's spiritual life. Parishioner and committee member Bob More is clear that "we are not the environmental club at the parish." He emphasizes that care for creation is a mission of the church that is grounded in faith. This commitment is clear in the spiritual dimension of the many activities they sponsor, in the establishment of prayer stations outdoors on church property, and in their encouragement of parishioners to set up sacred gardens and spaces at their homes.[24]

The CCH ministry is integrated with other churches and faith groups as well. Saint John Neumann took the lead in establishing a network of parishes with creation-care teams in the Arlington diocese, having interested ten to become active and another six to explore participation. They make use of programs and resources of the Global Catholic Climate Movement and the Catholic Climate Covenant to deepen their work and are in touch with other dioceses—for example, in Atlanta and San Diego—to learn about their programs.[25] The parish is also

22. More, Sabo, and Broderick, conversation with author.
23. More, Sabo, and Broderick, conversation with author.
24. More, Sabo, and Broderick, conversation with author.
25. More, Sabo, and Broderick, conversation with author.

active in a regional interfaith group that works on environmental issues. That group awarded St. John Neumann the Sustainability Champion Award in 2018 in recognition of its sustainability efforts.[26] Taken together, the efforts of the CCH committee at St. John Neumann constitute a comprehensive response to *Laudato Si'* that other congregations can emulate.

Meeting the Moment

Our world is facing a challenging set of decades ahead. Economies everywhere are colliding with the structural limits of the growth-driven, industrial model of development, creating disruptions to both environments and economies. Coming disorders will not be limited to the fierce rainstorms and firestorms that currently grab the headlines. The 2020 pandemic reminds us that, because environmental tentacles are everywhere, environmental impacts can pop up, whack-a-mole style, anywhere and anytime.

Governments need help responding to this moment. Local communities, including faith communities, need to be transformed and transforming, and ready to assist, and even lead where required. Religious institutions, congregations, and people of faith can commit to a host of actions: using renewable energy for power, heating and cooling, and transportation; reducing our use of goods or reusing or recycling them; treating eating as an act of justice and food as a sacred gift; greening investments and making them socially impactful; using lands with great care and with attention to their environmental and social payoffs; supporting pro-poor financial opportunities, and advancing professed values through purchases that are fairly traded, union friendly, and environmentally sound.

---

26. "Celebrating our Creation Care Teams," Catholic Climate Covenant, https://catholicclimatecovenant.org.

There is more, as changed faith communities and institutions introduce reforms well beyond those cited in this volume. We can walk, bike, and take public transport to church and elsewhere. We can create faith-based purchasing co-ops so that all faith communities across a region buy cleaning supplies and other products from vendors who sell only recycled, toxin-free products. We can support microfinance and enterprises that offer dignity to difficult-to-place workers. And we can call for an income floor that eliminates debilitating poverty and a ceiling that provides incentive for innovation without obscene levels of wealth.

Now imagine all these things done not as ends in themselves but for the greater glory of God. Each action emerges from prayerful discernment and is celebrated in prayerful gratitude. Liturgies give thanks for environmental and social healing; religious education classes teach care for creation rooted in the natural environment; parish social gatherings reclaim food as a sacred gift, not a commodity; liturgical seasons align with natural ones; homilies reveal the long-overlooked ecological richness of Scripture; reconciliation services open our eyes to unjust treatment of other communities, and some prayer practices become rooted in nature, like the Laudato Si' Chaplet.

Such a hearty, creative response can redeem this time of turmoil. As the old order crumbles, we need not scramble in a futile attempt to preserve decades-old unsustainable habits that have run their course. Our faith traditions offer inspiring visions of a better, more dignified and humane world. Why not create a new order that reflects the values we hold dear? Why not embrace this moment of gift, recognizing it as a path to the kingdom?

We can meet this moment, and, with God's help, we can transform the bleakest of prospects into a promising future. Our success, hard won, will be evident to all in the blossoming of a renewed Earth and the well-being of the once-poor.

Appendix I

The Sustainable Development Goals

1. No Poverty
2. Zero Hunger
3. Good Health and Well-being
4. Quality Education
5. Gender Equality
6. Clean Water and Sanitation
7. Affordable and Clean Energy
8. Decent Work and Economic Growth
9. Industry, Innovation, and Infrastructure
10. Reduced Inequalities
11. Sustainable Cities and Communities
12. Responsible Consumption and Production
13. Climate Action
14. Life below Water
15. Life on Land
16. Peace, Justice, and Strong Institutions
17. Partnerships for the Goals

Appendix II

Creation Flows from the Trinity

Saint Francis's poetic interpretation of creation is given powerful theological underpinnings by St. Bonaventure, the Franciscan scholar and doctor of the church who lived in the decades following Francis's death. In *The Mind's Road to God*, he lays out a rationale for finding God through creation, noting in summary form that "all creatures of this sensible world lead the mind to the eternal God."[1]

Why would this be true? The answer starts with Bonaventure's conception of the Trinity, helpfully explained by Franciscans Sr. Ilia Delio, OSF, Br. Keith Warner, OFM, and spiritual director, Pamela Wood.[2] In the Trinity, the Father's self-expression, the entire collection of God's ideas, is communicated as the Word (the Son); the Love communicated between them is the Spirit. Thus, the Trinity is the act of communication among Father, Son, and Spirit, a God of relationship whose idiom is love.

This communication of love is not a treasure reserved by and for the three persons of the Trinity; it is a gift directed generously outward as well. For Bonaventure, this outward expres-

1. Saint Bonaventure, *The Mind's Road to God*, trans., with an introduction by George Boas (Liberal Arts Press, 1953), chap. 2, no. 11.
2. Ilia Delio, OSF; Keith Douglass Warner, OFM; and Pamela Wood, *Care for Creation: A Franciscan Spirituality of the Earth* (Cincinnati: Franciscan Media, 2008).

sion of love is creation itself, making the universe "the speech of God." As the outward expression of God manifest all around us, nature is a pathway back to God.

Bonaventure's teaching that God can be found through nature carries powerful implications not often heard in Sunday sermons. If God is revealed through creation, it follows that "the first book of revelation . . . was the 'Book of Creation.'"[3] The natural world is a companion to Scripture in expressing the Word of God; indeed, every creature can be thought of as a "little Word" of God.[4]

Thus, creation is not a product that God manufactured and handed off to a distribution center; it is a living entity infused in an ongoing way with God's very Self. In *Laudato Si'*, Pope Francis marvels at the implications of Bonaventure's trinitarian theology: "The Franciscan saint teaches us that *each creature bears in itself a specifically Trinitarian structure*, so real that it could be readily contemplated if only the human gaze were not so partial, dark and fragile."[5]

3. Delio, Warner, and Wood, *Care for Creation*, 9.
4. Delio, Warner, and Wood, *Care for Creation*, 45.
5. Pope Francis, *Laudato Si'*, no. 239.

Appendix III

Building on the Franciscan Vision

If Saints Francis and Bonaventure insisted that kinship extends to all creation, two twentieth-century thinkers, Pierre Teilhard de Chardin, a French Jesuit, and Thomas Berry, a Passionist priest, set this relational perspective in the larger context of evolution.

Teilhard and Berry lauded Charles Darwin's great scientific insight that the natural world evolves over time.[1] But while Darwin's evolution unfolded within the boundaries of the biological world, Teilhard and Berry echo Francis and Bonaventure in seeing matter as infused with spirit throughout the universe. "Matter is not dead, but alive with divine immanence," is how Yale scholars Mary Evelyn Tucker and John Grim succinctly describe the perspective of Teilhard and Berry.[2] A spirit-infused material world suggests an evolutionary dynamic different from Darwin's: evolution is driven not only by mutations and natural selection but by a psychic energy as well—what Teilhard called love.[3] "Driven by the forces of love, the fragments of the world

---

1. Pierre Teilhard de Chardin, *The Human Phenomenon: A New Edition and Translation of Le phénomène humain*, trans. Sarah Appleton-Weber (New York: HarperCollins, 2015), 218.

2. Mary Evelyn Tucker, John Grim, and Andrew Angyal, *Thomas Berry: A Biography* (New York: Columbia University Press, 2019), 33.

3. Tucker, Grim, and Angyal, *Thomas Berry*, 204.

seek each other so that the world may come into being," Teilhard wrote.[4]

For Teilhard and Berry, the universe is not merely alive but imbued with direction and purpose. The universe unfolds toward ever-greater complexity, characterized by an expansion of consciousness. Indeed, over the history of the universe, a progression of increasing complexity, from atoms and molecules to cells, plants, and animals, has characterized its evolution, with humans at the pinnacle of consciousness to date. The purpose of this eons-long progressive advance in consciousness is union with God.

Berry draws out the profound implications of a spirit-filled and purposeful physical universe. It is radically different from the Cartesian worldview, in which humanity is separate from nature and where the nonhuman exists to serve the human. In the Cartesian worldview, which Berry labeled the "Old Story," the universe is essentially a workshop for human initiatives. The result is industrial societies that cleverly convert raw materials into goods for humanity and wealth for their makers while normalizing barbarities ranging from unswimmable rivers and empty fisheries to the extinction of species. Such perverse outcomes are "normal" only if we see ourselves as separate from nature. The human of the Old Story is like a child in a sandbox, busy experimenting and playing in a world of imaginative possibilities but largely unaware of her relationship to a larger, wondrous surrounding reality.

However, if we grasp the spirit-filled nature of the universe and the love that causes it to continually unfold toward greater consciousness, we understand the beauty of Berry's famous phrase, "the universe is a communion of subjects, not a collec-

4. Teilhard de Chardin, *The Human Phenomenon*, 188.

tion of objects."[5] We understand why he would write that "to wantonly destroy a living species is to silence forever a divine voice." In what Berry called the New Story, we see ourselves as part of a 14-billion-year cosmic, unfolding reality that is matter and spirit intertwined, and that draws us inexorably toward God. In this chronicle, the unfolding of the universe is not just a set of facts but an engaging story, a narrative that offers an all-encompassing worldview to situate us properly in the universe.[6]

5. Thomas Berry, *Evening Thoughts: Reflecting on Earth as a Sacred Community* (San Francisco: Sierra Club Books, 2006), 20.

6. Tucker, Grim, and Angyal, *Thomas Berry*, 100–101.

Bibliography

Books

Almond, R. E. A., M. Grooten, and T. Petersen, WWF. *Living Planet Report 2020: Bending the Curve of Biodiversity Loss.* Gland, Switzerland: WWF International, 2020.

Avila, Charles. *Ownership: Early Christian Teaching.* Eugene, OR: Wipf & Stock, 1983.

Berry, Thomas. *Evening Thoughts: Reflecting on Earth as a Sacred Community.* San Francisco: Sierra Club Books, 2006.

Boff, Leonardo. *Cry of the Earth. Cry of the Poor.* Maryknoll, NY: Orbis Books, 1997.

Bonaventure, Saint. *The Mind's Road to God.* Translated with an introduction by George Boas. Liberal Arts Press, 1953.

Brueggeman, Walter. *The Prophetic Imagination,* 40th anniversary edition. Minneapolis, MN: Fortress Press, 2018.

Catechism of the Catholic Church. www.vatican.va.

Cherlet, M., C. Hutchinson, J. Reynolds, J. Hill, S. Sommer, G. von Maltitz, eds. *World Atlas of Desertification.* Luxembourg: Publication Office of the European Union, 2018.

Clapp, Rodney, ed. *The Consuming Passion: Christianity and the Consumer Culture.* Downers Grove, IL: Intervarsity Press, 1998.

Compendium of the Social Doctrine of the Church. www.vatican.va.

Cross, Gary. *An All-Consuming Century: Why Commercialism Won in Modern America.* New York: Columbia University Press, 2000.

Dear, John. *The Beatitudes of Peace: Meditations on the Beatitudes, Peacemaking and the Spiritual Life.* New London, CT: Twenty-Third Publications, 2016.

Delio, Ilia, Keith Douglass Warner, and Pamela Wood. *Care for Creation: A Franciscan Spirituality of the Earth.* Cincinnati: Franciscan Media, 1999.

Gardner, Gary T. *Inspiring Progress: Religions' Contributions to Sustainable Development.* New York: W. W. Norton, 2007.

Grim, John A. *Indigenous Traditions and Ecology: The Interbeing of Cosmology and Community.* Cambridge, MA: Harvard University Press, 2001.

Grooten, M., and R. E. A. Almond, eds. *Living Planet Report—2018: Aiming Higher.* Gland, Switzerland: World Wildlife Fund, 2018.

IRENA. *Global Energy Transformation: A Road Map to 2050.* Abu Dhabi: International Renewable Energy Agency, 2019.

Meadows, Donella H., and Dennis L. Meadows, et al. *The Limits to Growth: A Report for the Club of Rome's Project on the Predicament of Mankind.* New York: Universe Books, 1972.

Merton, Thomas. *A Vow of Conversation: Journals 1964–1965.* Edited by Naomi Burton Stone. New York: Farrar, Straus, Giroux, 1988.

Morselli, Marco Cassuto, and Giulio Michelini, eds. *The Friendship Bible: Passages of the Torah-Pentateuch Commented upon by Jews and Christians.* Milan: Edizioni San Paolo, 2019.

Mumford, Lewis. *The Transformations of Man.* New York: Harper & Brothers, 1956.

Schoolmeester, T., and K. Verbist, eds. *The Andean Glacier and Water Atlas: The Impact of Glacier Retreat on Water Resources.* Arendal, Norway: UNESCO. GRID-Arendal, 2018.

Swimme, Brian, and Thomas Berry. *The Universe Story: From the Primordial Flaring Forth to the Ecozoic Era—A Celebration of the Unfolding of the Cosmos.* San Francisco: HarperSanFrancisco, 1994.

Teilhard de Chardin, Pierre. *The Human Phenomenon: A New Edition and Translation of Le phénomène humain.* Translated by Sarah Appleton-Weber. New York: HarperCollins, 2015.

Tucker, Mary Evelyn, John Grim, and Andrew Angyal. *Thomas Berry: A Biography.* New York: Columbia University Press, 2019.

World Commission on Environment and Development. *Our Common Future.* Oxford: Oxford University Press, 1987.

ARTICLES

Abbott, Allison. "Biodiversity Thrives in Ethiopia's Church Forests." *Nature* 565, January 29, 2019.

Blackmore, Willy. "The Boycott's Abolitionist Roots." *The Nation*, August 14, 2019.

Brown, Elizabeth Anne. "Widely Misinterpreted Report Still Shows Catastrophic Animal Decline." *National Geographic*, November 1, 2018.

DiCamillo, Nathan. "Bound by Faith and Thrift: The Double-edged Sword of Christian CUs." *American Banker*, March 30, 2018. https://www.americanbanker.com.

Dicastery for Promoting Integral Human Development. *"Aqua fons vitae*: Orientations on Water—Symbol of the Cry of the Poor and the Cry of the Earth." Vatican City: Dicastery for Promoting Integral Human Development, 2020.

Dudley, Nigel, and Sasha Alexander. "Agriculture and Biodiversity: A Review." *Journal of Biodiversity* 18, nos. 2–3 (July 28, 2017).

Eplett, Layla. "The Logistics of One of the Largest Langars." *Scientific American*, November 22, 2016.

Etzioni, Amitai. "The Crisis of American Consumerism." *Huffington Post*, December 6, 2017, www.huffpost.com.

Galey, Patrick. "Climate Impacts 'to Cost World $7.9 Trillion' by 2050." Phys.org, November 20, 2019.

Goodin, David K., Alemayehu Wassie, and Margaret Lowman. "The Ethiopian Orthodox Tewahedo Church Forests and Economic Development." *Journal of Religion and Society* 21 (2019).

Grant, Andrew, and Mike Coffin. "Breaking the Habit: Why None of the Large Oil Companies Are 'Paris-Aligned,' and What They Need to Do to Get There." Carbon Tracker, September 2019, carbontracker.org.

Hallmann, Caspar, et al. "More Than 75 Percent Decline over 27 Years in Total Flying Insect Biomass in Protected Areas." *PLOS ONE*, October 18, 2017, journals.plos.org.

Hu, Winnie. "A Billion-Dollar Investment in New York's Water." *New York Times*, January 18, 2018.

Hunt, Chelsie, Olaf Weber, and Truzaar Dordi. "A Comparative Analysis of the Anti-Apartheid and Fossil Fuel Divestment Campaigns." *Journal of Sustainable Finance & Investment* 7, no. 1 (2017).

Kramer, Katherine, and Joe Ware. "Counting the Cost 2019: A Year of Climate Breakdown." *Christian Aid*, December, 2019, www.christianaid.org.

Kumar-Rao, Arati. "India's Water Crisis Could Be Helped by Better Building Planning." *National Geographic,* July 15, 2019.

Li-Qing, Jiang, et al. "Surface Ocean pH and Buffer Capacity: Past, Present, and Future." *Nature Scientific Reports*, December 9, 2019.

Loy, David. "The Religion of the Market." *Journal of the American Academy of Religion* 65, no. 2 (1997): 275–90.

Ludescher Imanaka, Jessica, Greg Prussia, and Samantha Alexis. "*Laudato Si'* and Integral Ecology: A Reconceptualization of Sustainability." *Journal of Management for Global Sustainability* 5, no. 1 (2017).

Ludt, Billy. "IGS Solar Installing 2-MW Solar Project for DC Catholic Charity." *Solar Power World*, July 10, 2019, www.solarpowerworldonline.com.

Mangunjaya, Fachruddin Majeri, Chantal Elkin, Gugah Praharawati, Imran S L. Tobing, and Yeremiah R. Tjamin. "Protecting Tigers with a Fatwa: Lesson Learn Faith Base Approach for Conservation." *Asian Journal of Conservation Biology* 7, no. 1 (2018): 78–81.

Maros, Alexander. "The Ecological Theology of the Ecumenical Patriarch Bartholomew I." *International Journal of Orthodox Theology* 8, no. 1 (2017).

Mekonnen, Mesfin M., and Arjen Y. Hoekstra. "Four Billion People Facing Severe Water Scarcity." *Science Advances,* February 12, 2016.

Mikusiński, Grzegorz, Hugh P. Possingham, and Malgorzata Blicharska. "Biodiversity Priority Areas and Religions—A Global Analysis of Spatial Overlap." *Oryx* 48, no. 1 (2013): 17–22.

Ripple, William J., et al. "World Scientists' Warning of a Climate Emergency." *BioScience* 70, no. 1 (2020): 8–12.

Yuan, Wenping, et al. "Increased Atmospheric Vapor Pressure Deficit

Reduces Global Vegetation Growth." *Science Advances,* August 14, 2019, https://advances.sciencemag.org.

REPORTS

Anthropocene Working Group. "Results of Binding Vote by AWG." Subcommission on Quaternary Stratigraphy. International Commission on Stratigraphy, May 21, 2019, http://quaternary.stratigraphy.org/working-groups/anthropocene.

"Banking on Climate Change: Fossil Fuel Finance Report 2020." Rainforest Action Network, March 18, 2020, www.ran.org.

Bélanger, J., and D. Pilling, eds. "The State of the World's Biodiversity for Food and Agriculture." FAO Commission on Genetic Resources for Food and Agriculture Assessments Rome: FAO, 2019.

Breitburg, Denis, et al. "Declining Oxygen in the Global Ocean and Coastal Waters." *Science,* January 5, 2018.

Ceballos, Gerardo, Paul R. Ehrlich, and Rodolfo Dirzo. "Biological Annihilation via the Ongoing Sixth Mass Extinction Signaled by Vertebrate Population Losses and Declines." *Proceedings of the National Academy of Sciences.* July 25, 2017.

FAO, IFAD, UNICEF, WFP, and WHO. "The State of Food Security and Nutrition in the World: Safeguarding against Economic Slowdowns and Downturns." Rome: FAO, 2019.

Human Development Report 2019, http://hdr.undp.org.

International Union for the Conservation of Nature (IUCN). The IUCN Red List of Threatened Species. Version 2020-1. 2020, https://www.iucnredlist.org

IPBES. "Summary for policymakers of the global assessment report on biodiversity and ecosystem services of the Intergovernmental Science-Policy Platform on Biodiversity and Ecosystem Services." Bonn: IPBES Secretariat, 2019.

IPCC. "Summary for Policymakers." In *Climate Change 2013: The Physical Science Basis. Contribution of Working Group I to the Fifth Assessment Report of the Intergovernmental Panel on Climate Change.* Cambridge, UK: Cambridge University Press, 2013.

Kaza, Silpa, Lisa C. Yao, Perinaz Bhada-Tata, and Frank Van Woerden. *What a Waste 2.0: A Global Snapshot of Solid Waste Management to 2050*. Washington, DC: World Bank, 2018.

Leach, Melissa. "Inequality and Sustainability." In *World Social Science Report 2016*. Paris: UNESCO and International Social Science Council, 2016.

Millennium Ecosystem Assessment. "Ecosystems and Human Well-Being." Washington, DC: Island Press, 2005.

NCUA. "Strategic Plan: 2018–2022." January 25, 2018, https://www.ncua.gov.

REN21. "Overview of Energy Access." In *Renewables 2020: Global Status Report*. Paris: REN21 Secretariat, 2020.

V. Masson-Delmotte, et al., eds. "Summary for Policymakers." In *Global Warming of 1.5°C. An IPCC Special Report on the Impacts of Global Warming of 1.5°C above Pre-industrial Levels and Related Global Greenhouse Gas Emission Pathways in the Context of Strengthening the Global Response to the Threat of Climate Change, Sustainable Development, and Efforts to Eradicate Poverty*. Geneva: IPCC, 2018.

DOCUMENTS

Francis, Pope. *Laudato Si': On Care for Our Common Home*. Vatican City: Libreria Editrice Vaticana, 2015.

———. "*Querida Amazonia*: Post-Synodal Apostolic Exhortation of the Holy Father Francis to the People of God and to All Persons of Good Will." February 2, 2020.

John Paul II. *Centesimus Annus*. May 1, 1991.

"Joint Statement by the Islamic Foundation for Environmental & Ecological Sciences (IFEES/EcoIslam), Mosques & Imams National Advisory Board (MINAB), and the Bahu Trust on Divesting from Fossil Fuels and Investing in Renewable Energy." IFEES/EcoIslam, MINAB, and Bahu Trust. The Global Climate Divest-Invest Summit. September 10–11, 2019. Cape Town, South Africa, https://financingthefuture.global.

Paul VI, Pope. *Populorum Progressio: Encyclical Letter of Pope Paul VI on the Development of Peoples*. http://www.vatican.va.

Second Vatican Ecumenical Council. Pastoral Constitution on the Church in the World of Today, *Gaudium et Spes*.

Index